T0372594

Official Cambridge Exam Preparation

Complete

FIRST

Workbook
with answers
WITH AUDIO

Third edition

B2

Jacopo D'Andria Ursoleo
Kate Gralton

Cambridge University Press
www.cambridge.org/elt

Cambridge Assessment English
www.cambridgeenglish.org

Information on this title: www.cambridge.org/9781108903363

© Cambridge University Press and Cambridge Assessment English 2021

First published 2008
Second edition 2014
Third edition 2021

20 19 18 17 16 15 14 13 12

Printed in Dubai by Oriental Press

A catalogue record for this publication is available from the British Library

ISBN 978-1-108-90336-3 Workbook with answers with Audio

Contents

1 A family affair

Grammar

Present perfect simple and continuous

1 Complete the email with the correct form of the verbs in brackets. Use the present perfect simple or continuous.

From: Isabella
To: Mum
Subject: News from NYC

Hi Mum and Dad,

How are you? Sorry I **(1)** .... (not be) in touch sooner, but I **(2)** .... (organise) my new life in New York. As you can see, I **(3)** .... (change) my email address to the one at my new job. I **(4)** .... (stay) with my friend Angie since I arrived. I **(5)** .... (sleep) on her sofa and she **(6)** .... (help) me find an apartment to rent. I **(7)** .... (love) staying with her, but she just doesn't have enough space for me. The only problem is that all the apartments we **(8)** .... (find) so far **(9)** .... (be) either too expensive or very dirty. I'm sure I'll find a place soon, though. The bank I work at has thousands of employees so I might hear of something through them. The new job is very interesting and I **(10)** .... (spend) all week learning the new systems there. **(11)** I .... (go) out a lot in the evenings – I **(12)** .... (see) three Broadway shows since I got here! I **(13)** .... (decide) to slow down a bit now, though, as I **(14)** .... already .... (spend) too much money. I'll phone you at the weekend after I **(15)** .... (look) at some more apartments. Wish me luck!

Love, Isabella

2 On Saturday, Isabella's mum calls her. Use the prompts to write her questions using the present perfect simple or continuous.

1 you find / an apartment yet?

....

2 you visit / the Statue of Liberty?

....

3 you eat / healthily?

....

4 what Broadway shows / see?

....

5 you take / the subway everywhere?

....

3 Look at Isabella's diary. Write her answers to the questions in Exercise 2.

```
                                   June
9  Monday
   Buy monthly ticket
   at subway station
10 Tuesday
   Have dinner with
   Angie at  Joe's Burgers
11 Thursday
   Go to the theatre to
   see The Lion King – 8pm
12 Friday
   Visit the Statue of
   Liberty
13 Saturday
   Speak to Mum!
14 Sunday
   Appointment to view
   apartment – 2:30 pm
```

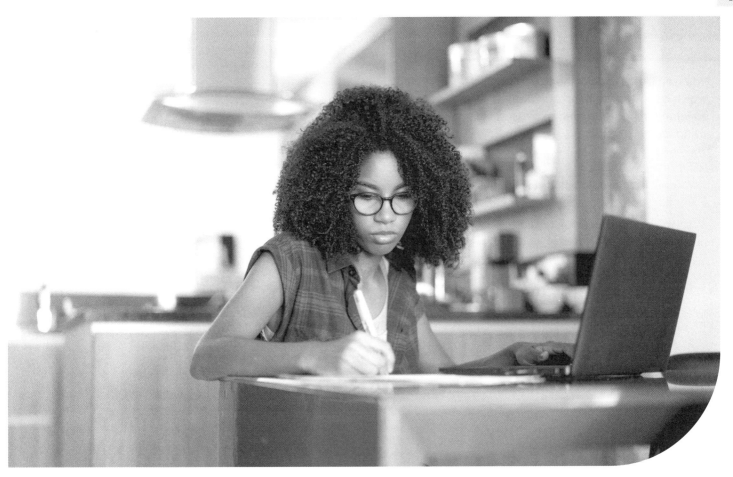

Vocabulary

Phrasal verbs

1 Match the phrasal verbs (1–6) with their definitions (A–F).

1 hang out	☐	**A** to arrive; to appear
2 count on	☐	**B** to become; to transform
3 turn into	☐	**C** to spend time with someone
4 make up	☐	**D** to invent
5 carry on	☐	**E** to continue
6 turn up	☐	**F** to rely on; to depend on

2 Complete the text with the correct form of the phrasal verbs from Exercise 1.

My classmate Jacopo and I were doing a course project together. We had to conduct a survey and then
(1) .... the information .... a report. I had already finished doing the survey, and we had arranged to meet at my house on Saturday afternoon to write the report. When Saturday came, he didn't **(2)** .... at the agreed time, so I phoned him. He **(3)** .... some story about being ill, but I was sure he just wanted to
(4) .... with his friends instead. I had to
(5) .... working on the project alone. I made sure that I didn't work with him again – I knew I couldn't
(6) .... him.

Collocations with *make* and *do*

3 Complete the sentences with the correct form of *make* or *do*.

1 My friend Anna doesn't have to .... any chores. She's so lucky!

2 Your hair is too long. You should .... an appointment at the hairdresser's.

3 John .... me a favour and drove me to the mechanic to pick up my car.

4 I always .... an effort to call my grandmother on Sundays.

5 If you want to .... a good impression at the job interview, you should wear a suit.

6 My clothes were getting really tight, so I .... more exercise and started eating healthily.

7 When I moved to a new school, I .... a lot of new friends.

8 There's no easy way to .... money. You just have to work hard.

9 I can't come to the picnic this afternoon. I haven't .... all my homework yet.

10 She needs to .... a phone call, but her battery is really low.

1

Listening Part 1

Exam advice

You won't hear exactly the same words as the words in the question, so listen for the same idea expressed using different words.

You will hear people talking in eight different situations. For questions 1–8, choose the best answer (A, B or C).

1   You hear a young man talking about his friend's new haircut.
    What was his opinion of it?
    A   It didn't look very attractive.
    B   It helped advance her career.
    C   It was a risky choice of style.

2   You hear a man talking to his daughter about meeting her mother for the first time.
    How did he react?
    A   He was upset by her behaviour.
    B   He was sympathetic to her problem.
    C   He was amused by something she said.

3   You hear a girl talking about getting driving lessons from her father.
    Why was she unsure about taking them?
    A   She was worried about failing the test.
    B   She thought her father might be impatient with her.
    C   She was concerned she would be a bad driver.

4   You overhear a man and a woman talking about a new café.
    What do they agree on?
    A   It needs a lot of customers to succeed.
    B   The service is very slow.
    C   There aren't enough tables.

5   You hear a woman talking about a tree in her neighbour's garden.
    What is the woman doing?
    A   offering a solution
    B   expressing anger
    C   asking for advice

6   You hear a husband and wife planning a holiday.
    What does the man insist on?
    A   going away for longer than usual
    B   returning to a place they've been to before
    C   having a holiday by the coast

7   You hear two friends talking about a photograph.
    How does the girl feel about her grandmother?
    A   She would like to have her approach to life.
    B   She wishes she had known her as a teenager.
    C   She wants to help her with her problems.

8   You hear a man talking about buying a new car.
    What is the most important factor for him?
    A   how reliable it is
    B   how big it is
    C   how much it costs

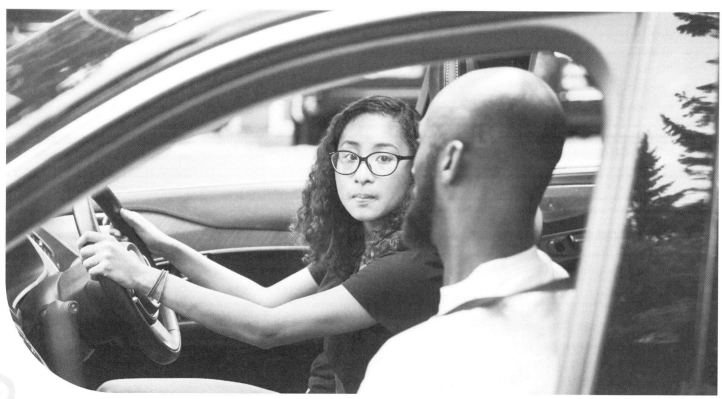

Reading and Use of English Part 2

For questions 1–8, read the text below and think of the word which best fits each gap. Use only one word in each gap. There is an example at the beginning (0).

Remember that it is very unlikely that you will need to use the same word twice in different gaps.

Exam advice

How many friends can you have?

Dunbar's Number **(0)** ......is...... the supposed limit to how many people you can maintain a social relationship with. In the 1990s, the anthropologist Robin Dunbar studied the social relationships of primates, **(1)** .... as monkeys and apes, and compared them to humans in terms **(2)** .... brain size and mental processing capacity. He concluded that for human social groups, 150 is **(3)** .... maximum number of people it is possible to have a stable relationship with. You may argue that you know more people, but according **(4)** .... Dunbar, it is highly unlikely that you could keep up real social contact **(5)** .... any more than this number. It has also **(6)** .... suggested in a recent study that Dunbar's number is applicable to online social networks and other communication channels. This is supported **(7)** .... the fact that the average number of Facebook friends is 150. But it seems that even **(8)** .... we have 150 friends on social media, we class only a small fraction of those as genuine.

Writing

Correct the spelling and punctuation in the school newspaper article. There are 15 mistakes. The first one has been corrected for you.

Remember to think about spelling and punctuation as errors can make what you write difficult to understand.

Exam advice

My sisters and I

I am so glad ~~Im~~ **I'm** not an only child. Of course, my parents are grate, but they don't always understand the problems of being young. Thats when I appreciete having sisters. I'm in the middle of two sisters and we spend all our time together They are my best friends and we get on really well. Of corse, we sometimes fight – for example, if I borrow a sister's cloths without permission or if our bedroom gets to messy. They are much tidyer than me! We do'nt usually have many problems, but if I argue whit one sister, there is always the other one to talk to? We have the same taist in music, too. I think that without my sisters', life would be very boring. would I like to have a brother, too? I'm not so sure. I think I like having sisters more.

2 Leisure and pleasure

Grammar

Making comparisons

1 Choose the correct option in *italics*.

1 I've heard it's going to be *too much hot / much hotter* tomorrow, so I want to go to the beach with my friends.

2 The crosswords in this newspaper are *much more difficult / much difficulter* than the ones online.

3 It's *more / much* challenging playing tennis with my sister because she's *a better / the best* player than me.

4 My grandmother bakes me *much more / more* cakes than I can eat.

5 Don't buy anything in this shop – the one further down the street is *much / more* cheaper.

6 Since I started taking the dog to obedience classes, he's been *far / more* easier to control.

7 I can cycle uphill *much faster / fastest* and *more easier / more easily* on my new bike.

8 I don't think his new songs are *as good as / as well as* the music on his first album.

2 Some of the sentences contain mistakes made by exam candidates. Underline the mistakes and correct them.

1 For me, a day of baking is as relaxing than a day at the beach.

2 You might like this book – it's the most interesting one I've read this year.

3 Playing football isn't as much expensive as playing golf.

4 I think the dog enjoys going to the park more when it's raining.

5 My brother is modifying his car so he can drive it even more faster.

6 The rules of chess are less complicated that you think.

7 Listening to music is many more enjoyable than watching television.

8 Walking to work is better for you than driving.

Adjectives with *-ed* and *-ing*

3 Complete the sentences with the correct adjective form of the words in brackets.

1 I find reading celebrity magazines extremely .... (bore)

2 I was .... to hear how much Mark spends on clothes. (astonish)

3 I'm .... about the dog – he hasn't eaten for a couple of days. (worry)

4 The student looked .... , so the teacher repeated the question. (puzzle)

5 Charlotte found it very .... when she scored a goal in her football match. (motivate)

6 I was .... that I forgot some of my dance steps on the night of the performance. (irritate)

7 I found the marathon absolutely .... due to the intense heat. (exhaust)

8 We are all very .... about going to Japan for our holiday. (excite)

4 Complete the table with the verb and noun forms of the adjectives.

Adjective	Verb	Noun
amused/amusing	to amuse	amusement
bored/boring		
confuse/confusing		
embarrassed/embarrassing		
excited/exciting		
exhausted/exhausting		
irritated/irritating		
motivated/motivating		
worried / worrying		

Vocabulary
Phrasal verbs and expressions

1 Match the phrasal verbs (1–8) with the definitions (A–H). Write the letters in the boxes.

1 come across ☐
2 come along ☐
3 come up against ☐
4 count on ☐
5 end up ☐
6 go on ☐
7 run out of ☐
8 throw yourself into ☐

A to be able to depend on something or someone
B to finally be in a particular place or situation
C to continue to happen or exist
D to start doing something with a lot of enthusiasm and energy
E to have to deal with a problem or difficulty
F to finish, use or sell all of something so that there is none left
G to meet someone or find something by chance
H to arrive or appear in a place

2 Complete the sentences with the correct form of the phrasal verbs in Exercise 1.

1 He started his blog as a hobby, but it .... becoming his job.
2 When I was cleaning out the cupboard, I .... my old ballet slippers.
3 My girlfriend has completely .... training for her first marathon.
4 If you have any questions about cooking, you can always .... your grandparents for advice.
5 I decided to go to a classical music concert, but it .... for so long that I got bored.
6 I was waiting for the bus but a taxi .... , so I took that instead.
7 The neighbours started building a swimming pool, but they .... money and had to stop.
8 When I started learning Spanish, I .... lots of problems, such as remembering the grammatical rules.

Listening Part 2

> Be careful: some of the words, phrases or numbers may seem to fit the gap, but are not correct. **Exam advice**

 You will hear a man called Michael Flannery talking about his work restoring and selling antique furniture. For questions 1–10, complete the sentences with a word or short phrase.

Restoring furniture

Michael's job restoring furniture was a **(1)** .... in the beginning.

Michael uses the word **(2)** .... to describe how his grandparents' furniture looked in his house.

Friends started giving him furniture that had been left in the **(3)** ....

Michael thinks many people dislike throwing away furniture they have no **(4)** .... for.

Michael quit working at a **(5)** .... to focus on his new project.

Michael started using **(6)** .... which he bought from other market sellers to decorate his stall.

Michael invested in a **(7)** .... so he could record his renovation projects.

There are over **(8)** .... people who regularly watch his online channel.

Michael knows it is unlikely that he will become a **(9)** .... doing this job.

A **(10)** .... has asked him to make a TV programme.

2

You are going to read part of an article about the hobby of scrapbooking. For questions 1–6, choose the answer (A, B, C or D) which you think fits best according to the text.

Don't choose an option just because you see similar words in the text and the questions. Make sure you understand the context.

Exam advice

Scrapbooking

For people who have never heard of scrapbooking, it's the practice of collecting everyday items and putting them into blank books in creative ways. I collect things such as tickets, receipts, menus and labels that most people would just throw away and I stick them in my books in artistic ways, with short written descriptions of what they are. It's the story of my family life, but told in a more visual way. It's a bit of a family tradition, in fact – I have similar books that both my mother and grandmother filled with recipes, photos and letters. My husband often tells me I should add more detail into my books, such as the stories behind the items, but I think pages and pages of writing can get a bit boring and it's a lot of extra work. Sometimes he'll help me stick things in if I want some company, and I think he enjoys it more than he admits, but I doubt he'll be starting his own book anytime soon.

My hobby helps me keep track of what's in my wardrobe, too. If I go shopping and buy a dress I really like, I'll paste in the price tag that comes with it, particularly if it's more expensive than usual, and maybe take a photo of me in
21 **it** and put that in. If I'm throwing away an old piece of clothing, I might save a button, or cut out a piece of the fabric to keep as a souvenir to remind me of how much I loved it. I suppose shopping for clothes is a hobby as well, so it's double the fun!

I would never claim that my work is innovative in any way, but I do find the whole process a real outlet for my creative energy. I experiment with different forms of handwriting and decorate the pages with glitter and stickers, too. If I go through the books I've put together over the years, I can see how my decorative approach has changed. I'm often surprised by how elaborate my work has become.

Sometimes when I look back, I realise that the decorative additions don't always completely suit the items that I've stuck in, but that's all part of the learning process.

My collection of scrapbooks is a wonderful family record. There are pictures of animals that are no longer with us, and a lot of birthday cards. My kids mostly love the ones that feature photos of them when they were little. I've kept some of their drawings, which are really funny and sweet. There are also some examples of their first attempts at writing, and I especially love looking at those. I fill a scrapbook every year and I really enjoy taking one down every now and again and looking through it.

Only one of my children has **followed in my footsteps** so 45 far. My daughter does online scrapbooking. She doesn't stick things in physical books, but she's got a fashion blog where she photographs clothes and shoes, and then creates beautiful pages to display them. She's the modern version of me, though I prefer a more hands-on approach, and I usually only go online to look at her blog. I think she'll end up working in the fashion industry, which is something I would have loved to do.

Everyone has a different reason why they enjoy scrapbooking. Some say it's like a kind of therapy for them – the chance to relive happy moments and forget about their everyday routine. But for me scrapbooking has really made me appreciate the day-to-day details that we don't normally keep a record of. Life isn't all holidays and celebrations, and pleasure is also found in the times that come between them. Keeping a scrapbook reminds me of that. It's lovely to look back at the memories, but it's essential to appreciate what's happening at the time. That's why I love the actual process of scrapbooking the most.

1 What does the writer say about her husband?
   A He doesn't get involved in scrapbooking.
   B He thinks scrapbooking requires too much effort.
   C He's considering taking up scrapbooking as well.
   D He thinks her scrapbooking could be improved.

2 What does 'it' refer to in line 21?
   A my wardrobe
   B a dress
   C the price tag
   D a photo

3 What does the writer say about her artistic style?
   A It has developed over time.
   B It's extremely original.
   C It's on the basic side.
   D It matches the content well.

4 Which scrapbook entries is the writer particularly fond of?
   A photos of her children when they were small
   B her children's drawings
   C things her children have written
   D pictures of old pets

5 What does the phrase 'followed in my footsteps' in line 45 tell us about the writer's daughter?

   A She uses the computer in the same way her mother does.

   B She enjoys making scrapbooks about shoes.

   C She has similar interests to her mother.

   D She will probably have the same job as her mother.

6 How can the writer's views on scrapbooking be summarised?

   A It's an effective means of relaxation.

   B It's a way of showing how special ordinary life is.

   C It's useful for keeping track of important occasions.

   D It helps pass the time when not much is going on.

Reading and Use of English Part 4

> In some cases there may be more than one correct answer but you should only write in one answer.
>
> **Exam advice**

For questions 1–6, complete the second sentence so it has a similar meaning to the first sentence, using the word given. Do not change the word given. You must use between two and five words, including the word given. Here is an example (0).

Example:

0 My father is older than your mother.

   OLD

   Your mother ....*isn't as old as*........ my father.

1 'Can you buy me a train ticket?' my mother said.

   ASKED

   My mother .... a train ticket.

2 This new recipe tastes much better than yours.

   NEARLY

   Your recipe doesn't .... as this new one.

3 I went to the shop because we didn't have any milk.

   RUN

   We had .... I went to the shop.

4 I've got more money than you, so let me pay.

   AS

   You don't have ...., so let me pay.

5 Without the extra tutoring, I wouldn't have passed the exam.

   BEEN

   I wouldn't have passed the exam if .... the extra tutoring.

6 I broke the vase by mistake.

   MEAN

   I .... the vase.

Writing Part 2

An article

> Remember to give your article a title and to organise your answer in a logical way using paragraphs.
>
> **Exam advice**

1 Join the two sentences into one sentence. Use *and*, *but* or *because*.

   1 Each week we go to a different place. We like to vary the landscapes we paint.

   2 I enjoy the company of the other artists. I create some lovely paintings, too.

   3 I would suggest it to others. It's a good opportunity to experience the natural environment.

   4 I didn't have much experience. The teacher taught me how to use colours and draw the outlines.

   5 I saw a poster advertising landscape painting lessons. I decided to enrol on the course.

   6 I would never give it up. I have made so many new friends and it helps me to be creative.

   7 I really love spending time outside. If it's raining, we paint in the studio.

2 Now look at the exam task and a student's plan below. Put the combined sentences (1–7) in Exercise 1 in the correct order in paragraphs (A–D).

> *My Outdoor Hobby*
>
> What is the hobby you do that gets you out in the sunshine?
>
> Include:
> - how you learnt to do it
> - why you enjoy doing it
>
> The winning article will be published in our online blog.

Student's plan:

A Paragraph 1: Introduction: Why and how I got started.
   Sentence ☐

B Paragraph 2: How I learnt to do it.
   Sentences ☐ ☐

C Paragraph 3: Why I enjoy doing it.
   Sentences ☐ ☐

D Paragraph 4: Conclusion: Would I recommend it to others? Will I continue doing it?
   Sentences ☐ ☐

3 Happy holidays?

Grammar

Past simple, past continuous, past perfect simple and past perfect continuous

1 Complete the story with the past simple or the past continuous form of the verbs in brackets.

I **(1)** .... (go) to bed early the night before because I **(2)** .... (know) I had a long day ahead of me. When I **(3)** .... (wake up), it **(4)** .... (rain) outside. I **(5)** .... (decide) to go anyway and just **(6)** .... (hope) the rain would clear. I **(7)** .... (hear) a forecast for better weather while I **(8)** .... (listen) to the car radio. The rain **(9)** .... (stop) at 6 am, just as I **(10)** .... (park) my car at the base of the mountain. While I **(11)** .... (get) my backpack out of the car, my friend Matt **(12)** .... (arrive). Both of us **(13)** .... (look forward to) the day ahead as we **(14)** .... (set off) up the mountain.

2 Choose the correct verb form in *italics*.

1 I *had driven / had been driving* for two hours when I decided to stop for lunch.
2 The plane *had already taken off / had already been taking off* by the time we got to the gate.
3 Before I went on this trip, I *hadn't travelled / hadn't been travelling* outside Europe before.
4 Our hotel room was too small because I *had forgotten / had been forgetting* to say I was bringing my children.
5 My dad was exhausted after playing golf because he *hadn't done / hadn't been doing* regular exercise.
6 We *had already paid / had already been paying* for a holiday in Spain when Ashley suddenly told me she wanted to go to the US instead.

3 Complete the text with the correct past form of the verbs in brackets.

My husband and I **(1)** .... (decide) to go on a cruise around the Greek islands because we **(2)** .... (work) really hard and needed to relax. The only problem was that by the time we **(3)** .... (realise) that we **(4)** .... (pack) all the wrong things, the ship **(5)** .... (sail). Even though the days were warm, the evenings were quite cool and we **(6)** .... (not bring) any warm clothes. I **(7)** .... (not take) my credit card with me, just a little cash. We **(8)** .... (feel) a bit stupid that we **(9)** .... (not plan) better. Luckily, I **(10)** .... (find) my credit card in my make-up bag while I **(11)** .... (get) ready one morning, so we **(12)** .... (buy) everything we needed on board.

at, in or *on* in time phrases

4 Complete the email with *at, in* or *on*.

From:	Mitchell Baker
To:	Lost Property Office, Charles de Gaulle Airport
Subject:	Lost wallet

My name is Mitchell Baker and I flew from London to Paris on Flytime Airlines flight FT753 (seat 24C) yesterday. The flight was **(1)** .... 7:35 **(2)** .... the morning I left my wallet in the pocket of the seat in front of me. I phoned the Flytime desk at Charles de Gaulle Airport and they told me the wallet had been found and was now at their Lost Property Office. I am still in Paris and staying at the Hotel Royale. I will be leaving **(3)** .... Friday and I cannot come to the airport to get my wallet until then. The driver for the airport bus at my hotel has offered to pick it up from you **(4)** .... the evening **(5)** .... Tuesday. His name is Philippe Ledoux and he will come to the office **(6)** .... 8 pm.

Yours sincerely
Mitchell Baker

Vocabulary
Travel words

1 Complete the crossword puzzle. Use the clues and the first letters of the words to help you.

Across

1 Mary often travels for work because she does a lot of b.............................. in India.

3 There are no evening flights, so you'll have to stay o.............................. in a hotel.

6 I really want to t.............................. to Africa.

7 Can you tell me the w.............................. to the train station?

8 Mark is away on a t.............................. to Scotland.

10 The word for h.............................. in the United States is *vacation*.

12 I like to go away for the w.............................. if I've had a busy week at work.

Down

2 If you go s.............................. in London, make sure you see Buckingham Palace.

4 The v.............................. I stayed in was very small – only about 30 people live there.

5 Ask your travel a.............................. if you have any more questions about the tour.

9 The j.............................. from Alice Springs to Darwin takes over 21 hours by bus.

11 He wants to live a.............................. somewhere so that he can experience another culture.

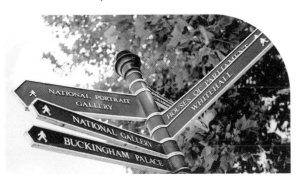

Suffixes

2 Complete the sentences with the adjective form of the noun in brackets.

1 Cinque Terre is famous for its coastal villages with very .... houses. (colour)

2 I think you can find more .... prices if you book your flights online. (reason)

3 My business trip was very .... – I got two new clients. (success)

4 You must be feeling very .... today if you want to go out in this weather. (energy)

5 I love the wonderful .... environment in the north of Canada. (nature)

6 My mother is rather .... and often travels abroad alone. (adventure)

7 He is .... that he will find a hotel room at this time of year. (doubt)

8 Going diving on the Great Barrier Reef would be a .... experience. (thrill)

9 It's important for all tourist attractions to be .... to wheelchairs. (access)

10 Don't go to Venice in July – it will be far too .... (crowd)

11 Why are you being so .... about where you're going on holiday? (mystery)

12 I've always found the people in New York very .... (friend)

Listening Part 3

> Don't choose your answers too quickly. Make sure you have listened to everything before you make your final decision.
>
> **Exam advice**

4 You will hear five short extracts in which people talk about a surprise they got on holiday. For questions 1–5, choose from the list (A–H) the main reason each person gives for why they were surprised. Use the letters only once. There are three extra letters which you do not need to use.

A I found what I was looking for.
B I made an important historical discovery.
C I recognised myself in something I saw.
D I had a very uncomfortable journey.
E I managed to surprise someone else.
F I was very upset by the situation.
G I had an unexpected encounter with someone.
H I was willing to be flexible.

Speaker 1 [**1**]   Speaker 4 [**4**]
Speaker 2 [**2**]   Speaker 5 [**5**]
Speaker 3 [**3**]

Writing Part 2

A report

> You can use paragraphs, headings and bullet points to make your report clearer.
>
> **Exam advice**

Read the Writing Part 2 task and answer. Then complete the report with the words and phrases in the box.

Transport report

Your class is planning a school trip to your capital city. The teacher has asked you to write a report on the advantages and disadvantages of travelling to and from the capital by train, and whether you would recommend it. Include the following information:

- the position of the station
- the cost
- the frequency of the trains

Write your **report** in **140–190** words in an appropriate style.

Although   Disadvantages   I would highly recommend
In addition   In terms of   It is also a benefit   The purpose of

Introduction

(1) .... this report is to provide information on train travel to London for the school trip. **(2)** .... advantages, the station is in a convenient position and ticket prices are reasonable. However, the trains are not very frequent.

Advantages

The stations in our city and in London are both in convenient locations: the local station is very close to the school, and the train will arrive in the centre of London. **(3)** .... that the cost is reasonable: a return ticket is £30 with a student discount. In comparison, the same return trip by coach would cost £35.

(4) ....

There is only one train to London a day and it leaves at 6 am. If any student misses the train, they cannot catch another one. **(5)** ...., to make sure there are enough seats for all students, tickets need to be reserved six weeks in advance.

Conclusion

(6) .... travelling to London by train for the school trip. **(7)** .... the trains are not very frequent, if the school books early enough it can be sure to get seats for all the students at a reasonable price.

Reading and Use of English Part 7

> Different texts or parts of the text may contain similar ideas, but you have to read carefully to decide which of these say the same thing as the questions.
>
> **Exam advice**

You are going to read an article in which four people describe their experiences on a cruise ship. For questions 1–10, choose from the people (A–D). Each person may be chosen more than once.

Which person

liked not having to change accommodation?	1
wasn't interested in socialising?	2
was anxious about not fitting in?	3
regretted a decision?	4
had to compromise?	5
didn't want to leave the ship during the cruise?	6
kept in touch with home?	7
was bothered by the weather?	8
felt the destination was unimportant?	9
used the time to complete a piece of work?	10

A Mary Jones

My husband, Bernie, and I are the same age, but I'm a lot less active than he is. We both like going sightseeing on holiday, but because of my arthritis I'm unable to walk very far these days. Cruises are a great way for us to spend time together – but do different things. We end up having completely different holidays even though we're travelling on the same ship. On the days we get into port, Bernie goes on shore for a change of scene, while I sunbathe on deck, chat to other passengers or find a comfortable spot to work on the novel I'm writing. When he shows me the photos of what he's seen and done that day, I try not to let it get me down. I'd love to go with him but there's only so much I can manage.

B Paul Fletcher

I'd never been on a cruise before, and I was a bit concerned that I'd be much younger than the other travellers. Well, I don't know whether it was the particular cruise I chose, but I needn't have worried. There were families with children, couples having a romantic break and groups of people around my own age, and there were plenty of activities for people to get to know each other and have a good time. When I needed to, I was able to find some quieter places to drop a line to friends to let them know how I was getting on. The ship even had a cinema! I enjoyed getting off at a different port every day. I'd been to some of the cities before, but never by sea. It was great not having to drive anywhere or constantly pack my suitcase up to go somewhere different.

C Chelsea Ryan

I was completely unprepared for the heat when I was planning my cruise. I knew it would be hot in August, though when we were at sea it was much cooler because of the sea breezes, but I never imagined that temperatures would be over 35 degrees when we were in port. As a result, I didn't leave the ship much when we got in to the various cities, but I got so fed up with staying behind that at one stop I decided to go on a group walk in the hills. There was a bus to take us up there, but once we arrived it was like an oven. Luckily, I wore a lot of sunscreen so I didn't get sunburnt, but it just wasn't worth getting off the ship for. I could have spent the day in the pool instead.

D Andy Simpson

I usually go on a ten-day cruise every year. I don't really care where I go, as long as it's somewhere hot. It may seem strange as there are so many other people on board, but I stay on the ship and use it as a kind of chance to get away from the world. I do so much volunteer work that I need an escape from everything when I'm on holiday. For me, going on a cruise is an opportunity to switch off for a while. I have yoga classes each day and I do a lot of walking around the deck listening to classical music. It's wonderful being on board, and I'm so comfortable it's preferable to stay there rather than go wandering about. I get a surprising amount of exercise – the fitness tracker I wear on my wrist told me I was doing 7,000 steps a day last time. I leave my phone at home and enjoy having time to myself.

4 Food, glorious food

Grammar

so and such, too and enough

1 Choose the correct option in *italics*.

1 Your children don't eat *so much / few / enough* healthy food.
2 There isn't *too many / enough / so few* flour to bake a cake.
3 The YouTube recipe was *too / so / such* fast to follow.
4 Your grandfather grows *such / few / so* delicious tomatoes.
5 This recipe has *too few / so little / too much* garlic that you can't taste it.
6 We both have *so much / so little / so few* opportunities to do any cooking.
7 That is *such a / so / such* good way of cooking eggs.
8 This lemonade isn't *much sweet / enough sweet / sweet enough* yet – let's add more sugar.
9 This steak is *too / enough / so much* tough to cut.
10 I saw *so much / so many / so little* cheap offers in the supermarket today.

2 Some of the sentences contain mistakes made by exam candidates. <u>Underline</u> the mistakes and correct them.

1 There are too much chemicals in processed food.
2 Many of the recipes in this book are traditional.
3 These strawberries have too much cream on them that I can't see them.
4 I don't think there is enough layers in the lasagne.
5 This recipe takes such a long time to make, but it's worth it.
6 My dentist says that I eat far too much sugar.
7 I didn't think the food in New York would be such expensive.
8 The service in this café is so slow – they don't make the coffee fast enough.

Vocabulary

Food and diet

1 Choose the correct option in *italics*.

1 You have a well-balanced *diet / food* – you always eat lots of fruit and vegetables.
2 The recipe for this *food / dish* is just too complicated.
3 You must come to my house for a *dish / meal* very soon.
4 The *dish / food* of the day on the menu is roast chicken.
5 I try to buy *organic / biological* food because I think it's better for my health.
6 My favourite type of *food / diet* is Italian – I love pizza!
7 If you eat *filling / strong* foods for breakfast, you can eat a smaller lunch.
8 I only buy fish when I can be sure it's *raw / fresh*.
9 I don't really like going out to restaurants for expensive *dishes / meals*.
10 He only cooks *fresh / simple* food, but it's always delicious.

2 Complete the crossword puzzle. Use the clues to help you.

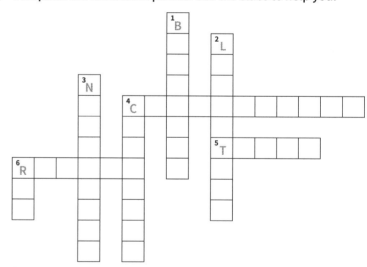

Across
4 Another word for fast food.
5 A word to describe food that is delicious.
6 Written instructions for how to cook a meal.

Down
1 The type of diet that has a wide variety of foods.
2 The way in which a person lives.
3 Food necessary for health and growth.
4 Providing food and drink at a social gathering.
6 A word to describe food that has not been cooked.

Reading and Use of English Part 1

For questions 1–8, read the text below and decide which answer (A, B, C or D) best fits each gap. There is an example at the beginning (0).

Try to guess what the answer is before you look at the options. You might know the answer already!

Exam advice

Example:

0 **A** learned   **B** taught   **C** said   **D** asked

What is umami?

We are **(0)** .... that there are four different tastes: sweet, sour, salty and bitter. However, Auguste Escoffier, the famous 19th-century French chef, talked about a fifth taste in his **(1)** .... , which he said was the **(2)** .... of his success. In 1909, the chemical basis of this taste was discovered by a Japanese chemist called Kikunae Ikeda. He was eating a bowl of seaweed soup and noticed that its delicious taste could not be **(3)** .... as any of the four accepted taste **(4)** .... He called this umami, which means 'delicious' in Japanese, and took his idea into the laboratory to find out **(5)** .... what it was. He discovered that the taste was caused by glutamate, which is a natural acid found in meat, fish, vegetables and dairy **(6)** .... When you cook meat, cheese ages or onions are fried, the glutamate breaks down and makes things taste **(7)** .... good. In 2002, this new taste was officially named umami in Ikeda's **(8)** ....

1	**A** cooks	**B** plates	**C** sauces	**D** kitchen
2	**A** secret	**B** idea	**C** reason	**D** mystery
3	**A** defined	**B** detailed	**C** decided	**D** designed
4	**A** boxes	**B** styles	**C** sections	**D** categories
5	**A** finally	**B** surely	**C** exactly	**D** mostly
6	**A** types	**B** objects	**C** products	**D** supplies
7	**A** widely	**B** particularly	**C** suitably	**D** virtually
8	**A** respect	**B** thanks	**C** approval	**D** honour

4

You are going to read a magazine article about relaxing while cooking. Six sentences have been removed from the article. Choose from the sentences A–G the one which fits each gap (1–6). There is one extra sentence which you do not need to use.

> **Exam advice**
> Read the whole text first so that you have a good idea of what it is about before you try to insert the missing sentences.

Cooking is therapy

Cooking can be a great way to relax after a tough day. Watching cookery programmes on TV is hugely popular nowadays, and according to psychologists, doing the cooking yourself with friends or family can ease anxiety and tension. But be careful: the kitchen can easily become a stressful place, so it's good to follow a few simple culinary rules.

First, enjoy the company of the people you are in the kitchen with. Use the time for conversation with your fellow cooks. **1 [ ]** This kind of discussion makes cooking fun. It's essential not to rush, so ensure you dedicate enough time to get the cooking done. Have the ingredients, equipment and recipe ready before you begin. This way you have less chance of forgetting an important stage, or running the risk of something burning while you are searching for the right wooden spoon to stir it. **2 [ ]** If you follow these carefully, you can relax in the knowledge you're doing it right. Clean up as you go, or you may end up getting stressed over the big mess there is to clean up at the end. If you keep everything in order, you'll be more relaxed.

Most importantly, keep your cool. **3 [ ]** These are inevitable. Good food takes time: think of how delicious the results will be in the end. Enjoy every moment of the preparation – cutting vegetables, mixing spices, stirring a pot. The cooking process needs to be joyful. **4 [ ]** And this will create even more stress. Take advantage of time in the kitchen to get rid of any worries or anxieties you have.

Be sure to make food you love eating, things you remember from your childhood that will warm your heart as well as your stomach. Alternatively, you can make healthy food to help you stay in shape. Whatever you cook, make sure you use fresh, high-quality ingredients. Start with basic foods, not products with lots of chemicals listed on the packet. **5 [ ]** Not only will they be tastier, but they will be better for you, too. Try to think about where the ingredients

have come from, how they are grown and when. Knowing the story behind what you are cooking with gives you respect for the producers of your food – where those apples were grown, who made your cheese and how. If you can, use local ingredients. **6 [ ]** This is because it hasn't caused carbon emissions due to transportation. Try to avoid waste and buy foods that have the least packaging. Make it your goal to throw away as little as possible.

Finally, turn off the TV and put on some of your favourite music. When your meal is ready, set the table, sit down with your friends or family, and really enjoy what you've prepared.

A Then you can be sure that your dishes will be pure and natural.	**E** Even if you're not familiar with all the ingredients, don't let this put you off.
B Don't panic if you experience setbacks or complications.	**F** If you cook when you're in a bad mood, you can't expect the results to be any good.
C Try watching a YouTube video that shows you all the steps.	**G** The nearer the food is to its source, the less impact it has on the environment.
D Share the tasks, explain what you are going to do next and chat about the different types of food you love.	

Listening Part 4

You will hear a radio interview with a man called Mike Jones, who has recently been a contestant on a TV cooking show. For questions 1–7, choose the best answer (A, B or C).

1 How did Mike feel about getting chosen for the show?
   A He was surprised because he hadn't applied.
   B He was sure that he would enjoy it.
   C He was worried that he would be too shy.

2 Mike has imagined working as a professional chef
   A because he spends so much time eating out.
   B as people have always enjoyed his food.
   C even though he has only recently started cooking.

3 Why did Mike make a cake on the first day of the show?
   A He knew the judges would love it.
   B He thought he had to cook something simple.
   C He was able to remember how to make it.

4 What did Mike find stressful about being on the show?
   A He couldn't concentrate because of the loud music.
   B He had to work in unfamiliar surroundings.
   C He didn't have enough time to cook.

5 How does Mike feel about being approached in the street?
   A He can't believe that anyone knows who he is.
   B He prefers it when it is children.
   C He likes the attention.

6 What does Mike think was the best thing about the whole experience?
   A His cooking skills have improved.
   B He has met a lot of people.
   C He has become even more interested in food.

7 Mike can't say whether he won the competition because
   A the final episodes haven't been filmed yet.
   B he wants it to be a surprise.
   C he isn't allowed to.

Writing Part 2

A review

Read the Writing Part 2 task and then complete the review with the words in the box.

Reviews wanted!

Have you been on a holiday that people who love food would really enjoy? Write a review of your holiday for our popular website. Describe where you stayed and what you did, and say why you think food lovers would enjoy it.

The best reviews will go on our website for travellers and tourists.

Write your **review** in **140–190** words in an appropriate style.

meals such recipes dish too so enough food

Last April, three friends and I flew from London to Pisa for a four-day foodie holiday in Italy. A 'foodie' is someone who loves good food. We stayed in a private villa in the Tuscan countryside with **(1)** .... beautiful views of the hills. My private room was warm and cosy, and decorated with antique furniture. I had to share the bathroom, but it was very clean and there was **(2)** .... hot water.

Every evening, we ate memorable **(3)** .... in the different restaurants in the village – all the ingredients were **(4)** .... fresh. During the day, our group of six people learned how to cook classic Italian **(5)** .... at the villa with the delightful Signora Elisa, and lunch was our own cooking creations. I couldn't believe I was eating a delicious pasta **(6)** .... each day that I had made with my own hands!

It was the perfect Italian cooking holiday for any foodie and I thoroughly recommend it. All the cooking lessons were included in the price, which made it a very good value trip. However, one word of warning. There's a lot of **(7)** .... to eat over the four days – possibly **(8)** .... much for some people!

5 Study time

Grammar

Zero, first and second conditionals

1 Complete the sentences with the correct form of the verb in brackets.

1 You would have more time to study if you .... (not be) always on your phone.
2 When I .... (go) to university, I'll live on campus.
3 He .... (need) to have a C1 level of English if he wants to study at Harvard University.
4 Meet me at the library as soon as you .... (finish) your lessons.
5 If you .... (choose) an apprenticeship, you get on-the-job training.
6 I can't hand in the project until you .... (complete) your part of it.
7 I .... (not do) any studying at home if I had a wide screen TV like that.
8 If you have problems doing the research, I .... (try) to help you with it.
9 Sit the exam again next semester if you .... (not pass) it the first time.
10 If I .... (get) a football scholarship, I wouldn't have to pay tuition fees.

2 Correct the mistakes in the highlighted parts of the sentences. Some of the sentences are correct.

1 I'm never able to concentrate on studying when the temperature goes over 35 °C.
2 If I were you, I'll spend more time practising speaking French than studying the grammar.
3 She has trouble finding a job if she leaves school at fifteen. But she's determined to do it!
4 He always wakes up in a bad mood when he studied too late the night before.
5 If I wanted to do engineering, will I need to take an advanced maths course at school?
6 Come on! If we're late handing this assignment in, the teacher will fail us again.
7 As soon as I finish this course, I was going to travel around the world.
8 If I lived in China for a year, do you think I'd be able to speak Mandarin by the end of it?

Vocabulary

Phrasal verbs

1 Replace the underlined words or phrases with the correct form of the phrasal verbs in the box.

> get away with   get over   hand back   live up to
> look back at   point out   put off   turn out

1 When I think about the time I spent at school, I only have good memories. ....
2 He managed to escape blame for breaking the classroom window. ....
3 Lauren always delays doing her maths assignments to the last minute. ....
4 When is the teacher returning our art projects? I want to show my parents mine. ....
5 I really try to be as good as my family's expectations of me. ....
6 After all that revision, it happened that the exam didn't count as part of my final mark anyway. ....
7 The lab assistant showed us that we weren't using the equipment correctly. ....
8 It took me a long time to recover from failing my piano exam. ....

find out, get to know, know, learn, teach and *study; attend, join, take part* and *assist*

2 The sentences below contain incorrect words. Replace them with the correct form of the words from the box.

> attend   find out   get to know   join   learn   study   take part in   teach

1 We should unite the university rowing club – we can get extra credits and get fit, too. ....
2 I have known a lot of tips for passing the exam from my maths teacher. ....
3 Mark has decided to learn veterinary science if his marks are good enough. ....
4 I can't assist all my lessons and continue working part time. ....
5 If you want me to take you to the train station, know what time the train leaves. ....
6 The work placement I did learned me a lot about the practical side of law. ....
7 Going to college social events is the best way to know a lot of people. ....
8 I really want to join the school play this year. ....

Study words

3 Complete the crossword puzzle. Use the clues to help you.

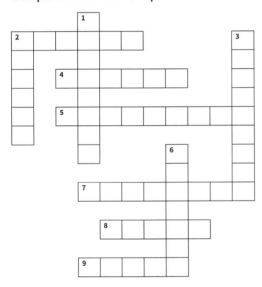

Across

2 I want to have a c................ in journalism. Do you think I need to go to university?
4 My sister did a d................ in marine biology and now she's a science teacher at a high school.
5 My parents don't think studying at art school will give me good job p................ .
7 I spend so much time studying new material, I don't have time to do r................ .
8 Why don't you get a t................ to help you pass your chemistry exams?
9 I can't believe I only got 58% in that test! I usually get much better m................ .

Down

1 Let's do our r................ for the project separately. I'll go to the library, and you do it online.
2 I thought history would be a really easy c................ , but I'm finding it difficult.
3 To gain a................ to study medicine at university you have to do well at school.
6 I had four English l................ a week when I was at school. I think that was too much.

Suffixes

4 Complete the table with the noun forms of the verbs in the box. Put six nouns in the 'other' column.

> advise   adjust   agree   assess   appear   behave   compare
> confuse   develop   exist   feel   intend   investigate
> involve   prefer   respond   qualify

-tion	-ence	-ment	-ance	other

5 Complete the sentences with nouns from Exercise 4.

1 I'm in complete .... with you – we should apologise to him immediately.
2 I'm tired of the constant .... with my twin sister. The fact that we look alike doesn't mean we're the same.
3 The government is starting an .... into the widespread cheating in state exams.
4 My brother loves maths but my .... has always been history.
5 I sent an email a week ago but I still haven't had a ....

5

Listening Part 1

6 You will hear people talking in eight different situations. For questions 1–8, choose the best answer (A, B or C).

In Listening Part 1, you will hear the context-setting sentence for each question. Use the time given to read the question and the options before you listen.

Exam advice

1 You hear a father talking to his son about university.
Why did the father leave university before he graduated?
- A He wanted to get married.
- B He failed his first-year exams.
- C He needed to start working.

2 You hear two students talking about the university library.
How does the man feel about using the library?
- A He gets frustrated that it takes so long to get the books.
- B He wishes it were easier to access the internet there.
- C He would go there more often if he had time.

3 You hear a student talking to a friend about his new school.
Why would he prefer to be at his old school?
- A He doesn't like being away from home.
- B He finds the classes at his new school too demanding.
- C He is missing out on opportunities.

4 You hear a student talking to a friend about a history report he has written.
Why does he want his friend to read it?
- A It's a project they have done together.
- B He wants to know if it is well written.
- C He knows she is good at history.

5 You hear a girl leaving a phone message for a friend.
Why is she calling?
- A to borrow some books
- B to ask for advice
- C to discuss a talk she has given

6 You hear two students talking about using tablets at school.
The boy says that tablets
- A are more economical in the long run.
- B are nicer to handle than books.
- C are easier to store at school.

7 You hear a man talking about a book.
What does he say about it?
- A It reminded him of his own life.
- B Someone encouraged him to buy it.
- C He had a feeling it would be good.

8 You hear a boy talking to a friend about studying after school.
What does he say about it?
- A He is easily put off by noise.
- B He often needs help with it.
- C He does very little schoolwork at home.

Reading and Use of English Part 3

For questions 1–8, read the text below. Use the word given in capitals at the end of some of the lines to form a word that fits in the gap in the same line. There is an example at the beginning (0).

Always check to see if an answer needs to be in a negative or a plural form.

Exam advice

A unique approach to learning

The Programme for International Student Assessment (PISA) is a worldwide study which has been measuring 15-year-old school pupils' scholastic (0) _performance_ in mathematics, science and reading since 2000. Finland has (1) .... performed highly on the PISA test and other nations are (2) .... in knowing why. There are some key (3) .... in how Finnish schools are run, starting with a high teacher-student ratio. To avoid having (4) .... and tired students, school doesn't start until 9 am., and the day ends relatively early, in (5) .... with other countries, usually after only two or three lessons with 20-minute breaks between them.

The overall system is not there to force (6) .... into students, but to create an environment of integrated learning which boosts collaboration and (7) .... They have the least amount of homework of any students in the world, spending an average of only half an hour a night on it. Finnish students do nearly all of their study at school in a low-stress atmosphere that puts an equal focus on acquiring (8) .... and growing as a human being.

PERFORM

REPEAT

INTEREST/DIFFER

MOTIVATE

COMPARE

INFORM

CREATE

KNOW

Writing Part 1

An essay

1 Read the exam question and the model answer.

> Everyone should stay in full-time education until the age of 18. Do you agree?
>
> **Notes**
>
> Write about:
> 1. preparing for working life
> 2. gaining knowledge
> 3. .... (your own idea)

In my country, young people only have to stay in education until the age of 16. <u>Some people think that</u> by this age they have studied enough but, <u>in my opinion</u>, it should be compulsory to study until you are 18.

<u>There are several reasons</u> for staying in full-time education. <u>Firstly</u>, the job market is increasingly competitive and so young people need all the advantages they can get. <u>Furthermore</u>, if you are not sure what career you would like to follow, staying at school gives you the time to discover what your passion is.

<u>However</u>, there are different types of education and knowledge. Young people could stay at school and study academic subjects such as maths and English but, <u>on the other hand</u>, they could do a training course where they learn more practical skills, like those needed to become a plumber or an electrician. Both of these options would give young people extra qualifications to put on their CV.

<u>To sum up</u>, <u>I believe</u> that young people should stay in education until they are 18, but they should be able to choose what skills they want to learn.

Read the task carefully. The essay may have a direct question or a statement which you have to give your opinion on.

Exam advice

2 Match the <u>underlined</u> phrases in the essay to the functions.

Giving your opinion

....

....

Introducing other people's opinions

....

Introducing an argument

....

Expressing contrast

....

....

Putting your ideas in order

....

....

Introducing your conclusion

....

3 Which statements about Writing Part 1 are True (T) and which are False (F)?

1 You don't have to do the essay in Part 1. T / F
2 You don't have to cover all three points in the question if you don't want to. T / F
3 Your essay must have headings. T / F
4 It's a good idea to use topic sentences to start each paragraph. T / F
5 You can express your personal opinions. T / F
6 You should use a variety of structures and vocabulary. T / F
7 You should try to write as much as possible. T / F
8 You should spend around 40 minutes on this part of the writing exam. T / F

6 Good job!

Grammar

Countable and uncountable nouns

1 Choose the noun in each group that is different. Write if that noun is C (countable) or U (uncountable).

1	(furniture)	sofa	bed	wardrobe	*U*
2	view	landscape	scenery	forest	
3	information	idea	knowledge	news	
4	advice	help	assistance	favour	
5	backpack	luggage	suitcase	handbag	
6	orchestra	instrument	music	concert	
7	sightseeing	travel	trip	transport	
8	meal	food	dish	course	

Articles

2 Complete the text with *a*, *an*, *the* or – (no article).

What if you don't want to go to university?

These days around 50% of **(1)** .... school-leavers in Britain go on to **(2)** .... university. So what do **(3)** .... other half do? Some enter **(4)** .... trade and do **(5)** .... apprenticeship to qualify for jobs such as **(6)** .... hairdressers or **(7)** .... electricians. Otherwise, they can find **(8)** .... job in three main areas: **(9)** .... selling of goods, either in shops or warehouses; **(10)** .... transport sector, which moves goods or people around; and **(11)** .... area of accommodation and food services. This range of industries has **(12)** .... huge number of vacancies for **(13)** .... young people. Often employees such as these later start **(14)** .... business of their own. In fact, as more and more people decide to go to university, it might be better to take **(15)** .... chance and get **(16)** .... experience doing **(17)** .... job that doesn't need **(18)** .... academic qualifications or leave you with **(19)** .... massive debt that young university graduates usually have.

Vocabulary

work or *job*; *possibility, occasion* or *opportunity*; *fun* or *funny*

1 Complete the conversation with the correct adjective in each gap.

Jake: How's the new job going?

Emily: Oh, it's absolutely **(1)** f............... . I'm working **(2)** p............... in an art gallery.

Jake: Lucky you. I'm working as a labourer on a building site. I do **(3)** m............... work like carrying bricks and cement around, and I'm working **(4)** o............... in the sun all day, so it's really **(5)** t............... . It's quite **(6)** w............... , though, so it pays the rent, but I'd love a job like yours, just standing around stopping people from touching the paintings.

Emily: That's not what I do. I work in a commercial gallery. We have a new exhibition by a different artist every month. I'm **(7)** r............... for making sure all the paintings are up on the walls before opening night. It's **(8)** h............... work.

Jake: I'd like to have a more mentally **(9)** c............... job like that. Do they pay you much?

Emily: Not really, and my boss can be quite **(10)** d............... . The artists are always behind in their work so it makes the job quite stressful. But it's all **(11)** w............... when the exhibition is ready and the opening night is a success. I'd like to do it as a **(12)** p............... job when I graduate.

2 Correct the mistakes in the sentences. Some of the sentences are correct.

1 I couldn't find any informations online about the company. ....

2 Come with me on Saturday – I'm going to a really fun party. ....

3 John backed his new car into a gate and the damage was quite bad. ....

4 If you get the possibility, call me tonight. ....

5 I spent all weekend doing geography homeworks. ....

6 Do you have any decorating equipments I can borrow? ....

7 I need an advice on how to prepare for a job interview. ....

8 Is there any opportunity you could babysit for me this evening? ....

Writing Part 2

An email or letter

1 Read the Writing Part 2 exam question and the model answer.

You see this advertisement on a job search website.

SHOP ASSISTANT WANTED

Computer World requires a part-time shop assistant for immediate start.

- Do you love technology?
- Do you have experience working in a shop?
- Can you communicate well in English?

To apply, write to the hiring manager, John Davis, explaining why you are suitable for the role.

Write your **letter** of application in **140–190** words.

Dear John,

I am writing to apply for the job of shop assistant which was advertised on your website.

I am very interested in technology and I am very good at using computers. I am studying computer science part time at university, so I think I would be able to answer questions from customers easily. I do not have experience of working in a computer shop, but I have been working as a shop assistant in a furniture shop for three years. There I serve customers and receive deliveries from the factory. I enjoy the job, but I would prefer to work for Computer World because it is more suited to my studies. I think I would be a very suitable person to work for you. Please contact me if you would like me to come for an interview.

See you soon.

Jennifer Alba

Did the candidate complete these requirements for writing a job application letter? Choose T (True) or F (False).

1 is within the correct word limit. T / F
2 is mainly in a formal style. T / F
3 is written in distinct paragraphs. T / F
4 has a correct formal greeting and sign off. T / F
5 opens with the reason for writing the letter. T / F
6 covers all the points in the advertisement. T / F

Exam advice

Think carefully about who the intended reader of your email or letter is and write it in an appropriate tone.

2 Match the beginning of the sentences from a job application letter (1–8) with the endings (A–H).

1 I am writing to apply for ....
2 The position was advertised ....
3 I am interested in the position because ....
4 My current position involves answering phones ....
5 I am an excellent communicator ....
6 I have experience using phone systems and ....
7 I have attached my CV and ....
8 I look forward ....

A to hearing from you.
B and enjoy interacting with clients.
C and welcoming clients at an architectural firm.
D on your website.
E I am available for an interview at any time.
F I have always wanted to work in hospitality.
G setting up external conference calls.
H the position of hotel receptionist.

6

Listening Part 3

Exam advice
Use the time given to read the options and <u>underline</u> the key words before the recording begins. You will then know what to listen for.

7 **You will hear five short extracts in which people talk about their first jobs. For questions 1–5, choose from the list (A–H) what each speaker says about their first job. Use the letters only once. There are three extra letters which you do not need to use.**

A It was an easy job to get.
B I felt lonely.
C It was sometimes quite boring.
D It kept me fit.
E I was paid well.
F It was too stressful to cope with.
G My qualifications were for a different job.
H I had to work at night.

Speaker 1		1
Speaker 2		2
Speaker 3		3
Speaker 4		4
Speaker 5		5

Reading and Use of English Part 5

Exam advice
The questions and the answers in the text are in the same order. After you have quickly read the whole text, find what part of the text each question is referring to and then read it carefully to eliminate the three incorrect options.

You are going to read an article by a headhunter, a person whose job it is to find new employees for companies. For questions 1–6, choose the answer (A, B, C or D) which you think fits best according to the text.

1 The writer suggests candidates add a paragraph to their CV to
   A distinguish themselves from other candidates.
   B highlight their previous achievements.
   C provide additional information about their career goals.
   D show their writing skills.

2 The writer recommends that applicants send their CV to a Human Resources department
   A so it can keep a copy on file.
   B because it will send your CV to the hiring manager.
   C only if clearly instructed to do so.
   D to help speed up the application process.

3 Why should you research a company before an interview?
   A To make sure you understand the precise role.
   B To enable you to show how much you know.
   C To reassure yourself that you are prepared.
   D To make certain you are able to ask detailed questions.

4 Asking about a company's problems at the interview shows that
   A you are keen to learn how you can help.
   B you already understand what they need.
   C you want to be in charge.
   D you are willing and adaptable.

5 Why is it impressive to explain the actions you'd take in a job?
   A It is unusual to do this in an interview.
   B It proves you don't need any training.
   C It shows you are confident about getting the position.
   D It is not an easy thing to do.

6 What is the most accurate summary of the final paragraph?
   A Often interviewers do not know what they are looking for.
   B If you make yourself the obvious candidate, you make everyone's task easier.
   C When you get the job, you will have to work even harder.
   D Interviewers want to see as many candidates as possible.

How to get that job

New York headhunter Carl Rogers gives us some advice

You may think that headhunters work solely for the employer, but they are also working for the future employee. Their goal is to make the best match between the candidate and the company that's looking to employ someone. As one of New York's leading headhunters, here is some advice I give to candidates to make them the obvious choice for the position they are competing for.

Look upon your CV not as a record of your past but as a statement of what you could do for that company in the future, if they employ you. Prepare a separate CV for every company you approach. Find out as much as possible about what the job requires, and then add a paragraph at the top of your CV that says how you will specifically do that job in a way that targets the needs of the manager you will be working for. That way, you will stand out as someone who will help the employer, not just someone who is looking for a job.

If you send your CV to Human Resources, the department responsible for the recruitment of new staff, it is highly likely that it will get lost or just filed away. We headhunters try to avoid HR departments as they can be inefficient. So should you. You need to go directly to the person who will be making the hire. If the job advertisement explicitly asks for a CV to be sent to HR, do it, but send another one to the manager who is making the ultimate decision for the job explaining what you've done. So while all the other candidates are still waiting to be interviewed by HR, the person who will make the final decision about who to hire already knows who you are.

So that you feel confident when you walk into the interview, you need to know not just about the position itself, but how it fits within the structure of the company. That means doing a lot of research beforehand. Learn about the company in greater depth than just reading the homepage of their website. Find out its challenges and goals, its culture and competitors, and all its products.

Now you are ready for the interview. Treat it as if it were the first day on the job. You are there to present a new project, which is 'the advantages of hiring you'. Turn the interview around by asking what problems the manager hopes to solve by employing you. They might start by giving you a list of your daily duties or tell you it is to replace someone who is leaving. You may have to make it clear that you are asking more about what they hope to gain from you as an employee, rather than just the day-to-day things they expect you to do. This demonstrates your extra enthusiasm and flexibility. When you get a clear idea of what it is they are looking for, such as higher profits or more clients, this is your moment to outline the steps you would take to do this. Show the manager how you think and work by suggesting what you would do to reduce costs or broaden the client base. Candidates are rarely so forward thinking in an interview and for this reason this strategy is very effective.

You will come across as a person who understands the job and is prepared to do it. Who doesn't want to employ someone who wants to solve problems and achieve goals? This is the fundamental reason for the interview. A company holds interviews so it can hire the best person for the job. Your interviewer will be delighted if that person turns out to be you – because then they can stop interviewing and get back to work.

Grammar

Infinitive and verb + -ing

1 Complete the sentences with the infinitive or -ing form of the verb in brackets.

1 Elisha has promised .... (show) me how to improve my golf swing.

2 I spend more time .... (sit) on the bench than actually playing volleyball.

3 Not .... (be) able to get away from work meant Jason missed a trekking trip.

4 My father got himself a dog .... (get) more exercise.

5 My son's fitness regime involves .... (train) three mornings a week.

6 These trainers have air pockets in them .... (reduce) impact.

7 She hasn't been playing tennis long enough .... (start) entering competitions.

8 The children amused themselves by .... (play) a board game.

9 .... (join) a walking club was a good way of making new friends.

10 The doctor warned me .... (not try) skiing again until I'd had physiotherapy.

2 Complete the sentences with the verbs in the box. There are two verbs which you do not need.

admitted   allowed   avoided   decided   expected
failed   reminded   succeeded   thought   warned

1 The cyclist .... using a type of bike frame that wasn't allowed in competitions.

2 He .... that joining a yoga class might help his back problems, but it only made them worse.

3 I .... to beat my best time when I last did a marathon, even though I won the race!

4 The photographer .... in finding the best position to get great shots of the finish line.

5 Luckily, I had been on the trail before, so I .... getting lost when my GPS stopped working.

6 The group weren't .... to ride their motorcycles through local villages because of the noise.

7 We had .... it to rain on the day of the tournament, but certainly not to hail!

8 The club .... to design a new uniform when they got a new sponsorship deal.

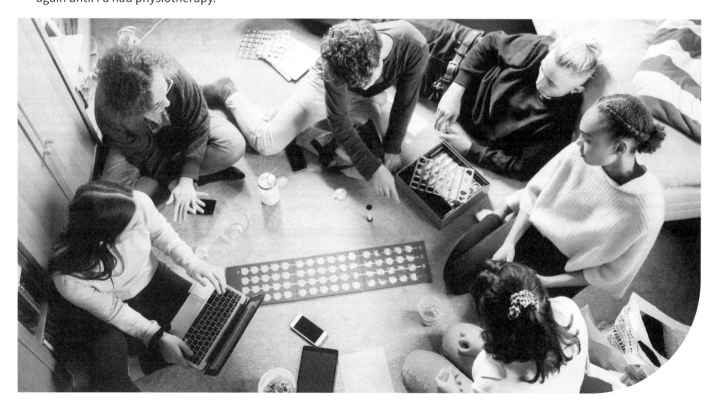

Vocabulary

Verb collocations with activities

1 Choose the correct option in *italics*.

1 I'm really looking forward to *going / playing* windsurfing when we're on holiday at the lake.

2 My dad has been *making / doing* a lot of exercise because he felt unfit.

3 Rachel is going to *compete in / play* a triathlon this weekend.

4 How long have you been *playing / doing* golf?

5 He didn't start to *do / play* weightlifting until he was 50.

6 The city has *held / done* the King's Mile Run every spring for more than 100 years.

look, *see* and *watch*; *listen* and *hear*

2 Complete the sentences using the correct form of *look*, *see*, *watch*, *listen* or *hear*. One of the answers is negative.

1 I managed .... the hole-in-one at the golf tournament because I was following that player.

2 I really enjoy .... Wimbledon on TV every year.

3 She .... the roar of the crowd as she overtook the lead runner.

4 If you .... to what the coach tells you, you'll never improve.

5 The umpire .... at the cricket pitch and decided it was too wet to play on.

6 There must have been 70,000 people .... the game at the stadium.

3 Correct the mistakes with *look*, *see*, *watch*, *listen* and *hear* in the sentences. Some of the sentences are correct.

1 Katherine saw at her watch to check what time it was. ....

2 You obviously weren't listening when I explained the rules of the game. ....

3 He could see the lead cyclist just ahead of him, so he started to pedal faster. ....

4 I can listen to music in the other room, but I don't know what song it is. ....

5 I watched Jack's car parked in front of the house, so I knew he was home. ....

6 She got up in the middle of the night because she listened to the baby crying. ....

7 Sophie doesn't usually watch TV in the morning – she reads the newspaper instead. ....

8 I watched she was busy talking to someone, so I waited to speak to her later. ....

Reading and Use of English Part 4

For questions 1–8, complete the second sentence so that it has a similar meaning to the first sentence, using the word given. Do not change the word given. You must use between two and five words, including the word given. Here is an example (0).

Example:

0 We didn't get lost because I brought the compass.

HAVE

If I hadn't brought the compass, we *would have got* lost.

1 The tour guide's suggestion was to take a different route down the mountain.

TAKING

The tour guide .... alternative route down the mountain.

2 Even though they had one less player, the team still won.

DESPITE

The team was able to .... one less player.

3 The risk of sharks meant very few people went swimming there.

SWAM

Hardly .... because of the risk of sharks.

4 What annoys me is people leaving rubbish on the forest trails.

FIND

I .... that people leave rubbish on the forest trails.

5 She survives on just four hours' sleep a night when she's sailing alone.

BY

When she's sailing alone, she .... just four hours sleep a night.

6 The doctor checked Michael's blood pressure before he went skydiving.

HAD

Michael .... by the doctor before he went skydiving.

7

Listening Part 4

Rather than focussing on individual words that you hear, think about the overall message.

Exam advice

You will hear an interview with a motorcycle racer called Darren Beanhill. For questions 1–7, choose the best answer (A, B or C).

1 Why did people laugh at Darren at his first ever race?
   A He was so young.
   B He had an old bike.
   C He wasn't very good.

2 Why is this year different for Darren from the last two?
   A His competitors know how good he is.
   B He's finishing first in some races.
   C He has changed his technique.

3 What does Darren say about his tyres this year?
   A They are different ones from last year.
   B He has more experience with them.
   C He still doesn't feel safe on the corners.

4 How does Darren feel about his lifestyle on tour?
   A He dislikes his accommodation.
   B He enjoys moving around a lot.
   C Being with his family relaxes him.

5 Darren says most professional motorcycle riders
   A aren't afraid of falling off their bike.
   B don't fully understand the risks.
   C are nervous about hitting other competitors.

6 What does Darren say about retiring?
   A He will give up racing as soon as he wins a championship.
   B He plans to make the decision with help from others.
   C He hopes to be able to keep going into his late thirties.

7 Darren says that racing in hot temperatures
   A gives him an advantage over other riders.
   B means he has to adapt his technique.
   C affects his bike's performance.

Writing Part 2

An article

Read the Writing Part 2 exam question and the model answer. Then complete the answer with the words in the box.

Use your own words, instead of repeating expressions taken from the question.

Exam advice

You have seen this announcement on an English-speaking website.

> **Someone I know that I really admire**
> Who is a person you know that you really admire?
> What have they done? What do you particularly admire about them?
> Write an article answering these questions. We will publish the best articles in our next edition.

Write your **article** in **140–190** words.

also   as a result   as well as   by doing this   in addition   moreover

My cousin Sam

A person that I really admire is my cousin Sam. **(1)** .... to being close in age, we grew up together because we live in the same town. Five years ago, Sam had a car accident. **(2)** .... he has to use a wheelchair because he can't walk.

Sam had always loved playing basketball and missed it very much. Then someone suggested he should try playing wheelchair basketball. **(3)** .... buying a special sports wheelchair, he did a training course to teach him how to play basketball sitting down.

He discovered that he loved the sport and he spent as much time as he could on the court. **(4)** .... he became very good, very quickly, and last year he was chosen to represent Britain on the wheelchair basketball team at the Paralympic Games. **(5)** .... he came home with a bronze medal!

I admire Sam because despite his injury, he decided to stay positive and find a way to enjoy life again. And by not giving up, he has **(6)** .... found great success – and that is why I am so proud of him.

8 Dream of the stars

Grammar

at, *in* and *on* to express location

1 Complete the sentences with *at*, *in* or *on*.

1 I saw Richard Randall .... stage .... the Victoria Theatre last year.

2 She was .... the cinema last night. I saw her .... the queue for popcorn.

3 The film industry .... India is called Bollywood.

4 There seems to be less drama and more comedy .... TV these days.

5 The actors have to be .... work and ready to start filming at 5 am.

6 His latest movie was filmed .... a small island off the coast of Scotland.

7 They first met .... an audition for a Broadway musical.

8 A lot of young actors live .... West Hollywood.

Reported speech

2 Read Jessica's question and write the words each person actually said.

> For my English class I am writing a review of the film Open Time. Can you tell me what you think of it?

1 Ashley told me she was going to see it next weekend.

2 Chloe said it was the funniest film she had ever seen.

3 Jack said he had never heard of it.

4 Olivia said she would definitely watch it again.

5 Connor told me he couldn't see it because he didn't live near a cinema.

6 Ryan said he hadn't really enjoyed it because it was too long.

1 Ashley: *I'm going to see it next weekend.*

2 Chloe: ....

3 Jack: ....

4 Olivia: ....

5 Connor: ....

6 Ryan: ....

Reporting verbs

3 Match the statements (1–7) with a reporting verb from the box.

> admit   agree   apologise   promise
> recommend   ~~remind~~   warn

1 Don't forget the show starts at eight.   *remind*

2 I'll be on time tomorrow.   ....

3 It was me who broke the mirror.   ....

4 I'm sorry I didn't see your performance yesterday.   ....

5 You should stream this TV series.   ....

6 You're right – we can go out tonight.   ....

7 Don't buy concert tickets from strangers.   ....

4 Now report what the people in Exercise 3 said.

1 *The drama teacher reminded us that the show started at eight.*

2 Oliver admitted that ....

3 My husband agreed that ....

4 Julia apologised for ....

5 William promised that ....

6 Angelo recommended that ....

7 Lisa warned us ....

8

Vocabulary

Describing entertainment

1 Complete the crossword puzzle. Use the clues to help you.

Across

4 Entertainment that is performed in a theatre.
5 When a story is very interesting and intense.
8 The actors perform on this in a theatre.
12 The people in the seats in a cinema or theatre.
14 Some actors become rich and ....
16 What you are on when a film is exciting. (4, 2, 4, 4)
17 Part of a film or play set in one place.
18 A play or a film that is based on songs or dancing.

Down

1 When an old TV show is repeated.
2 An unexpected direction in the plot of a film, play or book.
3 Another word for role.
6 When the end of the story is easy to guess.
7 He went to every .... of the play!
9 What a performer does in a play or film.
10 People watching a sporting event.
11 Watch multiple episodes without a break. (5, 5)
12 What an actor has to do to get a role.
13 A word to describe a film that is very funny.
15 Another word for *addicted*.

Listening Part 2

You will hear the individual words you need to put in the gaps, but you won't hear the sentences exactly as they are written. These sentences follow the same order as the information given by the speaker.

Exam advice

9 You will hear a woman called Margie Levine talking about her job as a Hollywood agent. For questions 1–10, complete the sentences with a word or short phrase.

> **Working in Hollywood**
>
> Margie was discouraged from getting into the entertainment business by her **(1)** ....
>
> Margie was told that work as a talent agent would suit her due to her strong **(2)** .... skills.
>
> Margie says she learnt a lot about the business because she worked at every **(3)** .... in her first company.
>
> Margie decided to start her own company so she could take on actors who didn't suit the **(4)** .... of her current employer.
>
> Margie quickly became successful because of the number of **(5)** .... she had.
>
> The more actors Margie sent on to casting directors, the more her **(6)** .... grew.
>
> Margie gives enthusiastic actors several **(7)** .... for becoming successful.
>
> Margie suggests that actors can prepare for future auditions by reading the latest **(8)** ....
>
> Margie believes that being **(9)** .... is the key to getting work.
>
> Margie recommends actors get their photos done by a **(10)** ....

Reading and Use of English Part 7

You are going to read an article in which four people talk about how they were famous for a short time. For questions 1–10, choose from the people (A–D). The people may be chosen more than once.

Remember that each of the 10 questions will only relate to one of the different sections of the text.

Exam advice

Which person

wanted fame from the beginning?	**1**		thought their reaction was natural?	**6**
was shocked to be offered an opportunity?	**2**		became famous through their own bad fortune?	**7**
knew that fame would be temporary?	**3**		regrets a missed opportunity?	**8**
blamed others for a failure?	**4**		benefited from someone else's absence?	**9**
didn't mind seeming foolish?	**5**		refused to comment on the situation at the time?	**10**

A Anna Simpson, 21

When I was 16, we lived on a busy road. One day I was standing at the garden gate when a car suddenly ran off the road and into a tree a few metres away from me. The car engine had caught fire and the woman at the wheel inside was unconscious. Without thinking, I raced around to the driver's door, but it was locked. I picked up a rock and smashed the window so I could open the door from the inside and pulled the woman out and away from the car. The media went crazy about what I'd done, but I didn't feel especially brave. Anyone would have done the same thing in my position. Journalists were trying to interview me, but I turned them all down. I really didn't want to have my face all over the news. I was just happy to hear the woman was recovering well in hospital.

B Mitchell Rice, 26

I often used to work as an extra on a soap opera filmed near my house. An extra is an actor who doesn't have a speaking role – I would just play a person on the street or someone in a café. It was quite good money for a student – I certainly earned a lot more than my mates. One day I turned up on the set and was handed a script. There was a new speaking role for a character to be filmed that day and the actor hadn't shown up. I never thought for a minute they'd ask me! It wasn't a big part, and they killed off my character after a few months, but the exposure I got meant people started to recognise me. I must admit I quite enjoyed the attention, but I didn't expect it to last, so I wasn't surprised when it all stopped after a few months. Of course, it meant that I could no longer be an extra in the show, but I soon found another job, in a restaurant this time.

C Theo Whitman, 31

When I was younger, I auditioned for a boy band in the hope of becoming the next big star, and amazingly I was one of the four people chosen. The whole selection process was made into a TV series, so I was in it right to the end and had become quite well-known even at that stage. After the selection process was over, the four of us went into the studio and recorded an album. The first song we released went straight to number one, even before we had time to shoot a video. That summer we went on tour around the country and performed to thousands of fans. But the record company chose really bad songs for us, so our album didn't sell all that well. They dropped us soon after. I wish they had given us more of a chance.

D Maisie Broadwood, 24

I was a bit of a lazy teenager, so sometimes I took the dog for a walk by holding onto his lead while I rode my bike at the same time. It was dangerous, but the dog loved it. One day I was cycling through the park and I noticed someone filming me on their phone. I turned and waved to them, but at the exact same moment the dog saw a squirrel crossing our path.
Well, you can imagine what happened … The dog chased after the squirrel and pulled me off the bike. A few days later the video of the accident went viral all over the world. I contacted the person who had posted it and we agreed that I would get part of the income, so I did well out of it. It's still on the internet, and people still watch it, but I'm not bothered about anyone laughing at me – it's paid for my university education.

Reading and Use of English Part 1

For questions 1–8, read the text below and decide which answer (A, B, C or D) best fits each gap. There is an example at the beginning (0).

Example:

0 **A** sounds   **B** suggests   **C** seems   **D** assumes

A forgotten star

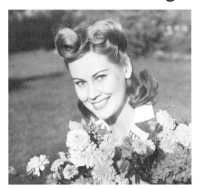

Gladys Sheerman (1918–2005) was a popular screen actress, but one who now **(0)** .... forgotten when we look back at the stars of the golden age of Hollywood. During her short career, her name **(1)** .... up twice for nomination for Best Supporting Actress – in 1941, for her successful debut in the comedy *House of Fire*, and again in 1950 for her **(2)** .... in the tragic Civil War drama *Mother Ann*.

Born in Queens, New York to a bus driver father and a waitress mother, she would spend hours at the cinema dreaming of a more exciting life. At the age of 18, with absolutely no acting **(3)** .... she moved to Los Angeles to **(4)** .... into the movie business. She was charismatic as well as beautiful, and landed her role in *House of Fire* in just two weeks after a **(5)** .... successful screen test. Her five **(6)** .... in films were all memorable, and she was well on her way to becoming a household name. Her career in Hollywood was cut **(7)** .... however, when she married the millionaire Miles Barton in 1952, who insisted she **(8)** .... from acting. The marriage lasted 50 years and produced five children – and she never acted again.

1	**A**	gave	**B**	came	**C**	took	**D**	looked
2	**A**	star	**B**	show	**C**	play	**D**	role
3	**A**	practice	**B**	experience	**C**	proof	**D**	trial
4	**A**	get	**B**	run	**C**	grow	**D**	turn
5	**A**	greatly	**B**	heavily	**C**	highly	**D**	deeply
6	**A**	appearances	**B**	exhibitions	**C**	presences	**D**	entrances
7	**A**	slight	**B**	small	**C**	short	**D**	low
8	**A**	end	**B**	quit	**C**	finish	**D**	retire

Writing Part 1

An essay

Read the Writing Part 1 exam question and the model answer. Complete the essay with words and phrases from the box.

In your English class you have been discussing social media and being famous. Now your English teacher has asked you to write an essay.

> Social media has made life more difficult for famous people. Do you agree?
> **Notes**
> Write about:
> 1. getting publicity
> 2. having contact with fans
> 3. .... (your own idea)

Write an **essay** in **140–190** words using all your notes and giving reasons for your point of view.

> because   because of this   for this reason
> one of the main reasons is   since   that is why

I think social media has definitely had an impact on the lives of famous people. **(1)** .... that they are able to get more publicity. Another is that they can have closer contact with fans. **(2)** .... , though, they may end up sacrificing their privacy.

Social media is now a key way for celebrities to promote themselves to the world. It's **(3)** .... that they post images of themselves in their homes with their families for everyone to see. They can use social media to show fans every moment of their lives and make them feel like they are personal friends. **(4)** .... fans are always hungry for more information about the people they admire, they love this glimpse into their glamorous existence.

However, being on social media means giving up a certain amount of privacy. **(5)** .... famous people are putting themselves at risk if they give out too much information, as some fans can become obsessed with them. Overall, though, I think social media has made life less difficult for celebrities **(6)** .... revealing their lives on social media can be a very easy way to get free publicity.

9 The power of the mind

Grammar

Modal verbs to express certainty and possibility

1 Rewrite the sentences in *italics* using *might, may, could, must* or *can't*. Sometimes, more than one answer is possible.

1 Look! He's got something behind his back. *It's my birthday so I'm sure it's a present for me.*
It's my birthday so he ...*must have a present for me*.....

2 Sandra's late coming home. *Perhaps she's out with her friends.*
She ....

3 He never says hello to me. *Maybe he doesn't speak English.*
He ....

4 She's doing an internship at a TV station. *That's bound to be fun.*
That ....

5 George doesn't have a licence. *It's definitely not him driving that car.*
It ....

6 Isabelle just won an award for bravery. *No doubt her parents were very proud of her.*
Her parents ....

7 Anna and Jack bought a house only six months ago. *I don't believe they have bought another one.*
They ....

8 I've tasted this recipe before. *Perhaps my mother cooked it for me when I was young.*
My mother ....

9 My great-grandmother signed her marriage certificate with an X. *I'm certain she wasn't able to write.*
She ....

10 I can't understand why I wasn't invited on the holiday. *It's possible they thought I couldn't afford it.*
They ....

2 Read the paragraph about thinking positively. Choose the correct option in *italics*. Sometimes, both options are possible.

If you've always woken up on Monday morning thinking that it **(1)** *mustn't / can't* be the start of another week already, you **(2)** *might / could* have been creating depressing feelings as a matter of habit. Wouldn't it be lovely to bounce out of bed and feel positive every morning? Think it **(3)** *can't / mightn't* be done? All it takes is some visualisation to boost your natural levels of serotonin before you go to sleep and you **(4)** *could / must* wake up feeling a lot more positive. When you visualise significant past achievements and happy moments in your life, the brain has difficulty distinguishing between what is real and what is imagined. It thinks the event **(5)** *must / can't* be happening now and produces serotonin. When you are in the middle of a stressful day, you **(6)** *may / might* be able to give your serotonin another boost if you take a few minutes to reflect on past achievements and happy memories.

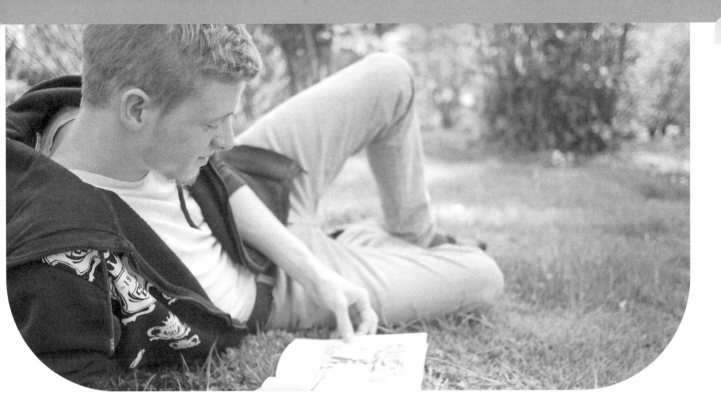

Vocabulary

achieve, carry out and *devote*; *stay, spend* and *pass*; *make, cause* and *have*

1 **Choose the correct option in *italics*.**

1 I love *spending / passing* my days off in the garden.
2 Why don't you *stay / spend* at home if you're feeling ill?
3 Humans blink so much we *spend / pass* two seconds a minute with our eyes closed!
4 I wish you wouldn't *stay / spend* so late at work every night.
5 I can't believe how fast the time has *spent / passed* on this holiday.
6 My parents used to *spend / pass* too much time watching TV, so they decided to give it away.

2 **Match the beginnings (1–6) with the endings (a–f) of these sentences.**

1 It seems scientists are making
2 The way you present yourself to the world has
3 It has taken a while but the government is now making
4 Think about whether your comments might cause
5 The constant changes in employment laws cause
6 I know you want to learn German quickly, but you have to have

a an impact on how people perceive you.
b patience or you will lose enthusiasm.
c great confusion in the workplace.
d an effort to tackle climate change.
e offence before you post them online.
f progress towards a cure for many diseases.

3 **Complete the table with the nouns in the box. One noun can go in more than one column.**

> an ambition   energy to   an improvement   an instruction   an objective
> an order   one's life to   research   success   a test   a threat   time to

achieve	carry out	devote

Reading and Use of English Part 4

Exam advice

Remember that the word given should not be changed in any way.

For questions 1–8, complete the second sentence so that it has a similar meaning to the first sentence, using the word given. Do not change the word given. You must use between two and five words, including the word given. Here is an example (0).

Example:

0 Please don't have the TV on too loud because I'm reading.

RATHER

I ......*'d rather you didn't*...... have the TV on too loud because I'm reading.

1 I don't think Michael has his phone switched on – it's not ringing.

BE

Michael's phone .... on – it's not ringing.

2 I found some old photos while I was up in the attic.

ACROSS

While I was up in the attic, ... some old photos.

3 This cake isn't nearly as tasty as the one you make.

MUCH

The cake you make .... this one.

4 'Don't you dare go into the shed!' my dad said to me.

WARNED

My dad .... into the shed.

5 This tai chi class won't finish before 6 o'clock.

GO

This tai chi class .... 6 o'clock.

6 It was a mistake for you to borrow the car without permission.

SHOULDN'T

You .... the car without permission.

Listening Part 1

Exam advice

The speakers will say things that relate to all three options in some way. Listen carefully to distinguish which one is the correct answer.

You will hear people talking in eight different situations. For questions 1–8, choose the best answer (A, B or C).

1 You hear a man talking about drinking coffee.

What's the main reason he prefers having coffee in a café rather than at home?

A He likes being motivated in the morning.

B He thinks the coffee in a café is superior.

C He only has the option of instant coffee at home.

2 You hear a father talking to his son.

Why does he want Jack to get out of bed?

A He thinks Jack should be doing more schoolwork.

B He wants to spend the day with Jack.

C He believes Jack should be using his time better.

3 You hear a woman talking about doing yoga.

What does she think people don't realise about yoga?

A how much effort it takes

B how relaxing it is

C how it affects your mood

4 You hear a man and a woman meeting after a long time.

How do they know each other?

A They used to do their shopping in the same place.

B They used to work together.

C They used to go to school together.

5 You hear a man talking about a favourite pair of trainers.

What's the problem with them?

A They don't fit him anymore.

B They're not suitable to wear every day.

C They're no longer the same colour.

6 You hear a man and a woman talking about a film they've just seen.

What do they agree about?

A how good one of the actors was

B how appropriate the music was

C how surprising the plot was

7 You hear a student who's worried about planning her study time.

What does she say about her situation?

A She shouldn't have a job while studying.

B She has to get her priorities right.

C She can't request study leave.

8 You hear a woman giving a talk about meditation.

What's the purpose of her talk?

A to describe how to meditate

B to suggest that more people should meditate

C to emphasise the benefits of meditating

Writing Part 2

A report

When you give recommendations in your report make sure that you include reasons for them.

Exam advice

Read the Writing Part 2 exam question and the model answer.

> Your English teacher has asked you to write a report on the parks in your town. Write about where the parks are, what people do in them and suggest ways in which they could be improved. Write your **report** in **140–190** words in an appropriate style.

Introduction

The aim of this report is to list the parks in my town, to say what people do in them and to suggest ways in which they could be improved.

Victoria Park

This is in the city centre between the shops and the station. It is quite small and is mainly used as a quick way to get from the station to the shops.

Riverland Park

This is a large park on the edge of town, with open grassy spaces and lots of trees. People come here to get some exercise or have a picnic with their families at the weekend.

Suggestions for improvements

Victoria Park has only one tree, and no grass at all. I would suggest planting more trees and adding an area of grass for people to sit on. Riverland Park has very old park benches, which are all broken. I suggest fixing or replacing them.

Conclusion

To sum up, the two parks in the city attract people for different reasons. Victoria Park needs to become a greener area, and Riverland Park needs to have some repairs carried out on the equipment.

1 Tick (✓) the sentences if the student has followed the suggestion in the report.

1 ☐ The report should have a title.
2 ☐ Each part of the report should have a clear heading.
3 ☐ The report should have an introduction and conclusion.
4 ☐ The introduction should not repeat the words in the question.
5 ☐ The report should not be written in an informal style.
6 ☐ The report should be between 140 and 190 words.

2 Choose the correct option in *italics*.

1 The purpose of this report is *finding / to find* out how many people are using the parks.
2 I would recommend *opening / to open* a kiosk near the picnic area.
3 I would also suggest *repairing / to repair* the old fountain in the centre of the park.
4 The best solution is *closing / to close* the park gates at night to prevent vandalism.
5 Another option would be *attracting / to attract* more people to the park by holding events.
6 My proposal involves *building / to build* a skatepark next to the basketball court.

10 Spend, spend, spend

Grammar

as and *like*

1. Some of the sentences contain mistakes made by exam candidates.
   Underline the mistakes and correct them.

   1 My father has worked like a mechanic all his life. ....
   2 As you can see from the size of the property, the family is very wealthy. ....
   3 I need a job that pays well enough for me to do things like go on regular holidays. ....
   4 These jeans are just as my old ones, but more comfortable. ....
   5 As much as I think the painting is beautiful, I can't justify paying so much for it. ....
   6 He works at the same company as I do. ....
   7 These shoes cost the same like the ones you can buy online. ....
   8 Who do you look as in your family? I'm told I have my mother's eyes. ....

Modal verbs to express ability

2. Complete the sentences with *can*, *could* or the correct form of *to be able to* and the words in brackets. Sometimes more than one answer is possible.

   1 I .... (not) come shopping with you tomorrow – I've got a dental appointment.
   2 I .... (not) follow a budget when I first started working and got into debt quite quickly.
   3 I .... carry the shopping in from the car if you need some help.
   4 It was due yesterday, but I .... (not) pay the electricity bill yet. I've been too busy.
   5 By the time your father was 18, he .... (already) support himself through his acting work.
   6 .... (I) build furniture to sell by the end of this woodworking course?
   7 She .... paid for it by now if she had saved a small amount of money each week.
   8 Let's ask James – I .... (always) rely on him to help out if I'm low on cash.

Vocabulary

arrive, *get* and *reach*

1. Choose the correct word in *italics*. In one sentence more than one answer is possible.

   1 As soon as she *arrived / reached / got* in Marrakesh, she headed to the street market.
   2 After driving for about an hour, they finally *arrived / reached / got* the shopping centre.
   3 Will the guests be *arriving / reaching / getting* in the morning or the afternoon?
   4 If I can *arrive / reach / get* to the bank in time, I can cash this cheque.
   5 If he *arrives / reaches / gets* at work late again, he might lose his job.
   6 I want to wrap the presents before the children *arrive / reach / get* home.

2 Complete the conversation with the words in the box.

available   bargain   brand   competitive   consumer   counter   debit card   purchase   sale   stock

Shop assistant: Can I help you?

Shopper: How much is this shirt? I can't find the price tag anywhere.

Shop assistant: It's on the inside. Look, here it is – £50. But all the shirts on this rack are half price, so it's only £25.

Shopper: That's a real **(1)** .... then. I wouldn't expect a shirt from this company to be so reasonable. It's normally such an expensive **(2)** ....

Shop assistant: Well, it's half price because our summer **(3)** .... is on at the moment. But even the regular prices are very **(4)** .... in this store. Our customers want quality, but they're also looking for value for money. We always try to listen to **(5)** .... opinion.

Shopper: Perhaps I should buy more than one then. I haven't seen any other colours, though.

Shop assistant: I'm afraid only the white ones are still **(6)** .... At the beginning of the season, we had five different colours, but they were incredibly popular and now they're all out of **(7)** ....

Shopper: That's a shame.

Shop Assistant: Would you still like to **(8)** .... this one?

Shopper: Yes, but if everything is half price, I think I'll keep on looking around – I might find something else I'd like to buy.

Shop Assistant: Certainly. Just bring whatever you choose up to the **(9)** .... when you're ready.

Shopper: Great. By the way, can I pay with a **(10)** .... here? If I decide to buy a lot of things, I probably won't have enough cash.

Shop Assistant: Yes, we accept all forms of payment here.

Phrasal verbs

3 Complete the text with the correct option in *italics*.

During my last university holidays, my dad agreed to let me work with him in his ice cream shop over the summer so I could make some money. The shop caters **(1)** *for / at* holidaymakers and as our seaside town pulls **(2)** *out / in* quite a crowd over the summer, it's always busy. I was there to take **(3)** *over / up* at the counter when Dad was out back making the ice cream or if he needed to pop **(4)** *into / over* the wholesalers to pick **(5)** *up / at* more ingredients. It was hard work and I was really worn **(6)** *out / in* when we closed up the shop at night. At first, Dad kept a close eye on me, always wanting to know what I was **(7)** *up / at* to, and we came **(8)** *up / over* against the problem of all my friends wanting free ice cream. But after a few weeks he cut **(9)** *up / down* on the criticism and I really started to enjoy hanging **(10)** *in / around* with him. We would chill **(11)** *out / over* together at the end of the day and come **(12)** *up / at* with new ideas for ice cream flavours. I think I'll do it again next summer.

Reading and Use of English Part 2

For questions 1–8, read the text below and think of the word which best fits each gap. Use only one word for each gap. There is an example at the beginning (0).

Augmented reality shopping

Whether **(0)** ....*you*......... buy online or physically go into a shop to get something, you still don't really know exactly how it's going to fit **(1)** .... your home until you bring it through the door. This is particularly true for large purchases, such as furniture, electrical goods, big pieces of artwork and **(2)** .... on. With augmented reality shopping, you can see **(3)** .... an item will look like in a space, or **(4)** .... if it will actually fit, without **(5)** .... to wait for it to arrive.

All you need to do is go into the online catalogue of a store, tap on the item you're interested in buying and select the augmented reality option. Then hold the smart phone in **(6)** .... of where you want the item to go in your home. And **(7)** .... it is! The yellow sofa you have **(8)** .... thinking about buying is in the room with you – well, on the screen of your smart phone, at least.

Listening Part 4

11 **You will hear a radio interview with a personal shopper called Amanda Houseman. For questions 1–7, choose the best answer (A, B or C).**

1 Amanda says that the main goal of a personal shopper is
  A making life easier for people.
  B selling expensive clothes.
  C deciding what people should wear.

2 What experience did Amanda get before becoming a personal shopper?
  A She worked for a stylist.
  B She studied at university.
  C She had a position as a sales assistant.

3 Amanda was able to become a personal shopper because
  A she was recommended to people.
  B she left the job she already had.
  C she asked someone to give her a chance.

4 Amanda selects clothes for new clients by
  A meeting them in their own environment.
  B observing how they dress.
  C using her imagination.

5 How has Amanda reacted to a problem with a client?
  A She now purchases less valuable items for her clients.
  B She is now more careful in her choice of clients.
  C She now asks her clients for payment in advance.

6 The reason Amanda prefers shopping without her clients is that
  A she wants to be the only one choosing the clothes.
  B she would only be able to choose clothes for that particular client.
  C she might have to stop the client choosing the wrong clothes.

7 What advice does Amanda give to potential personal shoppers?
  A Be sure of yourself and the client will trust your judgement.
  B Select a wide variety of clothes for each client.
  C Be prepared to have your suggestions rejected.

Writing Part 2
A review

Read the Writing Part 2 exam question and the model answer.

You see this announcement in an English language magazine.

Book reviews wanted

Have you read a book which had a cover that attracted you? Write a review of the book describing what it was about, and why the cover attracted you. Say whether you think other people would enjoy this book, too.
The best reviews will be published in next month's edition.

Write your **review** in **140–190** words in an appropriate style.

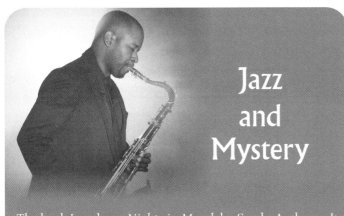

Jazz and Mystery

The book I read was *Nights in March* by Sandy Ambrose. It was the cover of the book that first attracted me. There was a picture of a man playing a saxophone. I'm learning this instrument at the moment, so that's the reason I bought the book. What I found out when I started reading it was that the man on the cover is the main character.

The book is set in New Orleans in the 1950s and is a collection of short stories about a local policeman called Miles who solves crimes during the day and plays in a jazz band at night. It was the description of life in New Orleans that made the stories very colourful and exciting.

What I really liked about this book was that it combined mystery with interesting facts about music and jazz musicians. Each story had an unexpected conclusion, so it was always surprising. I would recommend this book to everyone, but particularly to busy people who can read only for short periods of time. What I want to read next is the sequel to this book, *Nights in April*.

---

1 How does the writer say these things in the review? Find the phrases in the text.

1 I read *Nights in March* by Sandy Ambrose.
   ....*The book I read was*.... *Nights in March* by Sandy Ambrose.

2 The cover of the book first attracted me.
   .... first attracted me.

3 I found out when I started reading it that the man on the cover is the main character.
   .... the man on the cover is the main character.

4 The description of life in New Orleans made the stories very colourful and exciting.
   .... made the stories very colourful and exciting.

5 I liked that this book combined mystery with interesting facts about music and jazz musicians.
   .... combined mystery with interesting facts about music and jazz musicians.

6 Next, I want to read the sequel to this book, *Nights in April*.
   .... the sequel to this book, *Nights in April*.

2 Put the words in order to make cleft sentences.

1 tablet / moment / really / I / What / the / a / is / need / new / at
   ....

2 who / Michael / It / shop / the / from / book / was / stole / the
   ....

3 job / happens / character / his / What / is / loses / main / the
   ....

4 a / last / loan / was / out / she / year / bank / took / It / that
   ....

5 which / the / most / It / liked / I / shoes / was / black / the
   ....

6 is / time / department / don't / What / opens / the / know / I / store / what
   ....

11 Medical matters

Grammar

Relative pronouns and relative clauses

1a Complete the sentences with *which*, *who*, *whose* or *where*. Sometimes more than one answer is possible.

1 Often the foods .... are the least healthy are the most delicious.

2 The medical professional .... job it is to analyse blood samples is called a phlebotomist.

3 The athletes .... have the most success are those with the greatest determination.

4 The types of snacks .... he prefers to eat contain a lot of calories.

5 I love visiting places on holiday .... I know there won't be many tourists.

6 There aren't many houses .... have central heating here because of the warm climate.

7 The city's football team .... is at the top of the league has more fans than any other.

8 These days there are lots of people .... jobs don't provide them with any exercise.

9 People .... get regular medical check-ups are at less risk of illness.

10 The PE lessons .... my son does at school include gymnastics and rugby.

1b Add commas to the sentences in Exercise 1a that contain non-defining relative clauses.

1c Which relative pronouns can be replaced by *that*? Underline the pronouns.

1d Which relative pronouns can be omitted? (Circle) them.

2 Match the beginnings (1-6) with the endings (a-f) of these sentences.

1 People who have been professional athletes ....
2 The medicine I was taking last year ....
3 His chocolate cake, which he gave me the recipe for, ...
4 I'm trying to find out where ....
5 My cousin, who is a champion sprinter, ...
6 My husband has been told he needs to lose weight, ...

a I can do early morning yoga classes.
b which he has been trying to do for years anyway.
c really cleared up my skin.
d probably has a lot of calories in it.
e is coming here for a race next week.
f should keep doing exercise after they retire.

Vocabulary

Words relating to health

1 Complete the crossword. Use the clues to help you.

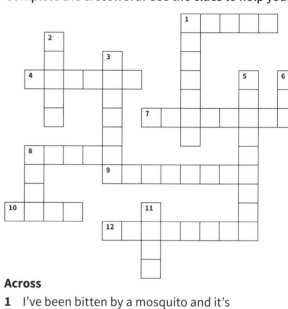

Across

1 I've been bitten by a mosquito and it's so i............................ .
4 The bus stopped suddenly and she b............................ her head.
7 I think I'm getting a cold – I've been s............................ all morning.
8 I b............................ my leg skiing and was in plaster for six weeks.
9 If my son eats peanuts, he gets an allergic r............................ .
10 David works hard as a nurse. He's always run off his f............................ .
12 Chloë's chest infection is much better but she's still c............................ .

Down

1 I gave up playing football because I was getting i............................ every week.
2 A bee s............................ her on the toe while she was walking across the grass.
3 I don't think I'll go to work today. I'm feeling a bit under the w............................ .
5 That chicken has gone off. Don't eat it – you might get food p............................ .
6 She seems to have a stomach b............................ . She feels like throwing up.
8 John cut his hand and it b............................ for a long time.
11 The babysitter tripped over some toys and h............................ her knee.

44

Word formation

2 Write the noun forms of the adjectives.

1 able .....*ability*.....
2 aware ....
3 certain ....
4 experienced ....
5 formal ....
6 happy ....
7 helpful ....

8 honest ....
9 patient ....
10 possible ....
11 predictable ....
12 reliable ....
13 satisfied ....

3 Complete the table with the negative forms of the adjectives from Exercise 2.
One adjective has two negative forms.

dis-	im-	in-	un-

Listening Part 3

You will hear five short extracts in which people are talking about medical conditions they had as a child. For questions 1–5, choose from the list (A–H) the effect that the condition had on them. Use the letters only once. There are three extra letters which you do not need to use.

The speaker may mention something related to more than one of the options. Listen carefully the second time to understand why only one option is correct.

Exam advice

A   They refused to do something.
B   They weren't believed at first.
C   They suffered because of the reaction of others.
D   They were to blame for the problem.
E   They have had the problem again.
F   They were forced to change their plans.
G   They passed the condition on to another person.
H   They only found one way to relieve a symptom.

Speaker 1 [ ] **1**

Speaker 2 [ ] **2**

Speaker 3 [ ] **3**

Speaker 4 [ ] **4**

Speaker 5 [ ] **5**

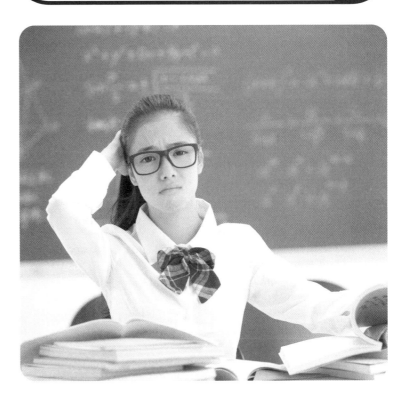

You are going to read an article about the use of medicinal herbs in the past. Six sentences have been removed from the article. Choose from the sentences A–G the one which fits each gap (1–6). There is one sentence which you do not need to use.

Exam advice

If you can't decide on a sentence for a gap, don't spend too much time thinking about it. Skip it and return to it after you have completed the others. You will then have fewer sentences left to choose from.

Medicine in the Dark Ages

Most of Britain was occupied by the Romans for nearly 400 years, and when the last of them left 1,600 years ago to defend Rome itself from hostile tribes, the remaining inhabitants were left to take care of themselves. The six hundred years of unrest and invasion that followed were known as the Dark Ages. **1** [ ] The Roman way of life, with its economic and social structures and its scientific knowledge, was quickly forgotten.

2 [ ] These were preserved and continued in religious communities such as monasteries, now the only source of medical care. Unsanitary living conditions throughout the land

meant frequent deaths from lung infections; wounds and skin diseases were common; and due to a limited diet, digestive diseases caused by a lack of nutrients were typical. Contagious diseases, such as leprosy, tuberculosis and possibly even a form of malaria, were also widespread.

All monasteries had a medicinal plant garden attached to their farms. **3** [ ] The monks would mix combinations of these into medicines to be consumed or rubbed into the body. In many cases, mixtures of different herbs were used to manage the 'humours', according to the theory of the ancient Greek physician, Hippocrates.

4 [ ] It was believed that if a patient took different combinations of herbs, this would balance the humours and cure the patient.

For example, if someone had a fever, they were diagnosed as having too much blood or yellow bile, and therefore required a cooling herb, such as sage. This had been brought to Britain by the Romans, who called it *salvia*. **5** [ ] Camomile flowers were used in herbal teas as a relaxant and to help with digestive problems, and were rubbed on the skin to treat infections. The leaves and yellow flowers of the comfrey plant were used to help cure broken bones and stop internal bleeding. Pennyroyal was used to combat the effects of poison.

A multitude of different plants was used to cure illnesses and diseases, and many of them are still recognised today as being effective. The Romans may have left Britain, but the legacy of their medical practices remains. **6** [ ] Even today when we have a camomile tea for a good night's sleep, or use mint to freshen our breath, we are following practices left by the Romans.

A They were filled with a variety of herbs and plants used to treat different illnesses.

B Roman doctors stayed in Britain so that they could continue to help people.

C The idea was that the body required the four bodily liquids – blood, mucus, yellow bile and black bile – in equal measure.

D They were continued by the monasteries for nearly 1,000 years, right up to the beginnings of modern medicine.

E However, it seems that one of the few areas of knowledge that survived the departure of the Romans was their medicinal practices.

F They used it in medicine and also ate it with lots of onions and garlic.

G Towns were abandoned and people returned to a completely rural existence.

Writing Part 1

An essay

Read the Writing Part 1 exam question and the model answer. Then complete the essay with the words and phrases from the box. Sometimes more than one answer is possible.

In your English class you have been discussing health. Now your English teacher has asked you to write an essay.

People don't look after their health properly these days. Do you agree?

Notes

Write about:

1. the effects of technology
2. leisure time / free time
3. .... (your own idea)

Write an **essay** in **140–190** words using all the notes and giving reasons for your point of view.

---

although   but   despite   due to   even though
however   whereas   while

I believe people are not as healthy as they were 50 years ago **(1)** .... changes in lifestyle that are not good for them. However, because of advances in science we are still able to live longer **(2)** .... living unhealthy lives.

(3) .... they make many tasks easier, smart phones and computers often cause stress because people are expected to be constantly available. Medical technology has, **(4)** .... , enabled easier diagnosis and treatment for conditions such as heart disease and cancer.

Fifty years ago, most jobs meant being on your feet, **(5)** .... most of us now sit down all day. **(6)** .... in the past leisure time was for resting, now we use it for getting the exercise we no longer do when we are at work.

What we eat and how it is prepared has also changed in the last 50 years. **(7)** .... we know much more about health and nutrition, much of the food we eat is processed and low in nutrients.

In conclusion, I think nowadays people have less healthy lifestyles. We should not rely on advances in technology to make us live longer, **(8)** .... increase our levels of exercise and consume more nutritious food instead.

It's important that your essay is well-organised, so make a plan before you start writing.

Exam advice

1 Complete the second sentence so it has a similar meaning to the first sentence, using the word given. Use between two and five words.

1 Despite the fact that they know they need to do regular exercise, many people spend most of their evenings on the sofa.

SPITE

Many people spend most of their evenings on the sofa, ... they need to do regular exercise.

2 You shouldn't spend too much time in the sun, although it's important to get plenty of vitamin D.

WHILE

.... get plenty of vitamin D, you shouldn't spend too much time in the sun.

3 Although they know it's bad for them, a lot of people eat too much junk food.

EVEN

A lot of people eat too much junk food, ... it's bad for them.

4 Due to temperatures dropping in winter, more people get illnesses such as colds.

FACT

Due to .... in winter, more people get illnesses such as colds.

12 Animal kingdom

Grammar

Third and mixed conditionals

1 Read about how Margie became a vet. Complete the sentences with the correct form of the verbs in brackets.

1 If I .... (not go) for a walk in the park that day, I .... (not find) the baby fox.

2 I .... (not seen) the advertisement for volunteers if I .... (not take) the fox to the wildlife sanctuary.

3 I .... (not discover) my passion for animals if I .... (not offer) to help.

4 I .... (not be) a vet today if I .... (not quit) my old job.

wish, *if only* and *hope*

2 Complete the sentences with *wish*, *if only* or *hope*.

1 .... I had remembered to lock my bicycle, it wouldn't have been stolen.

2 We .... you'll come to the music festival with us.

3 I .... we could talk for longer, but I have to pick my brother up from school.

4 My friends are arriving in an hour, so I .... there isn't much traffic on the way home.

5 I .... you had a good time at the zoo today.

6 It was exhausting painting the house alone – I .... you had been here to help me.

7 .... I could afford a horse. I would ride it every day.

8 I .... to get into university so I can study to be a veterinary nurse.

9 The dog needs more exercise – I .... you would take it for a walk occasionally.

10 I .... someone had told me hamsters were nocturnal. Mine keeps me awake at night!

3 Correct the mistakes in the sentences about a safari holiday. Some of the sentences are correct.

1 If only we had sat at the front of the truck, we would have got better photographs.

2 If Sarah hadn't the binoculars with her, we wouldn't have spotted the black rhino.

3 We saw lots of giraffes, but I wish had seen more elephants.

4 If we had gone the day before, we would have seen a family of lions.

5 There weren't any zebras today, so I hoped we see some tomorrow.

6 The guide said if we had come in July, we would have seen many more animals.

7 If only it didn't rain on the last day, the truck wouldn't have got stuck in the mud.

8 It's been a great holiday. I wish we could stayed longer!

Vocabulary

avoid, prevent and *protect*; *check, control, keep an eye on* and *supervise*

1 Choose the correct option in *italics*.

1 We need to *protect* / *avoid* the environment from too many tourists visiting at any one time.

2 All groups should be *supervised* / *checked* to stop them going into prohibited areas.

3 The fences are high to *control* / *prevent* people from getting into the animal enclosures.

4 You should *prevent* / *avoid* making too much noise when the animals are nearby.

5 Sheepdogs *control* / *supervise* the sheep when they need to be moved to a different field.

6 If you want to swim in the sea, it's a good idea to *check* / *avoid* when there are fewer jellyfish.

7 I've got a rash on my arm. I will *keep an eye on* / *supervise* it and call the doctor if it doesn't get better.

Reading and Use of English Part 7

You are going to read an article in which four people talk about their experience of looking after an animal. For questions 1–10, choose from the people (A–D). The people may be chosen more than once.

Which person

has an animal that is becoming more independent?	1
is not sure whether their actions are helpful?	2
imagined that looking after the animal would be easier?	3
is a different person from what other people imagine them to be?	4
understands that their animal will decide to leave?	5
originally got the animal so people would notice them?	6
is helping their animal return to its natural environment?	7
tells very few people about their animal?	8
feels what they are doing is urgent?	9
discovered their animal needed to be watched?	10

Remember that all the different sections of the text are used at least once, and that some are used more than once.

Exam advice

A

Bridie Foreman

I sometimes work in the garden with my ball python, Kylie, around my shoulders, so my neighbours see me as the crazy snake lady. But I'm not crazy. It was the teenage me that bought Kylie 20 years ago, and the now sensible grown-up me would never consider getting a snake. Yes, I didn't know they lived that long either! I think that when I got Kylie, I was looking for attention. I used to walk along the beachfront with her around my shoulders and I loved the reaction I got. I would often have a small crowd of curious people around me asking questions. I don't show her off so much these days, and she mostly stays in her cage inside. No one at work knows about my pet – I don't want my colleagues to think I'm strange.

B

Jamie Ross

I thought that having a ferret would be less time consuming than having a dog because it wouldn't need to go for walks. What a mistake that was! This is an animal that constantly demands your attention. You don't need to take it outside for walks, but it should be outside its cage for about four hours a day. It has a crazy amount of energy for exploring, and if I don't keep a close eye on it, my ferret can get into a lot of trouble very quickly. Ferrets have a habit of digging into their food, spilling their water dishes, knocking things down from shelves, digging up your potted plants… I think you see what I mean. It's a lot like having a small child.

C

Ashura Otieno

I work at the animal nursery connected to Nairobi National Park. Two years ago, we found a very young giraffe who was either orphaned or abandoned. His name is Yaro and he is probably one of the most popular of our rescued animals – he has even got his own website. These days he spends most of his time outside in the park, but comes back to us in the evenings or is kept inside for his own safety on days when there are lions around. Sometimes he comes across wild giraffes when he is out, and he is slowly building up the confidence to approach them. We hope that one day Yaro will choose to join them permanently, but we are giving him all the care he needs until he takes the next steps to living a wild life.

D

Felicity Callan

I work in a marine biology research facility. My current work involves studying seahorses to find out why they are disappearing from reefs around the world at such frightening speed. To do this, I had to capture a seahorse from the wild and bring it into the lab for observation. It's a lot of work just to keep the seahorse alive and I plan to put it back into the wild when our studies are over, but I still feel guilty about having it there in the first place. I know, though, that we need to take drastic measures if we want to save them from disappearing. They are such beautiful, delicate creatures and their natural environment is going through very destructive changes. I don't know if my work will make any difference, but I'm doing everything I can.

Reading and Use of English Part 1

For questions 1–8, read the text below and decide which answer
(A, B, C or D) best fits each gap. There is an example at the beginning (0).

Look carefully at the words that come before and after each gap. Some of these may typically be used with one of the options.

Exam advice

Example:

0 **A** says   **B** creates   **C** makes   **D** sings

The Kookaburra

The Kookaburra is a native Australian bird which **(0)** .... a call that sounds **(1)** .... like human laughter. The name comes from the Aboriginal word *guuguuburra*, which is used by the Wiradjuri people and means 'the sound of laughing'. A full chorus of kookaburras is a common sound in the **(2)** .... mornings and evenings in the eastern regions of Australia.

Kookaburras are commonly found in diverse habitats, **(3)** .... from forests to savannahs, which are a type of meadow. Unlike other species of bird, Kookaburras do not need to live by water. Fish do not **(4)** .... a major part of their diet. Instead, they typically **(5)** .... on other animals, such as insects and snakes.

Adults can grow up to 50 cm in height, **(6)** .... the female is usually bigger than the male. The male kookaburra can be easily **(7)** .... from the female by the blue feathers on its wings and its darker coloured tail. They have been known to live for as long as 20 years and **(8)** .... with the same partner for life.

1 **A** exactly   **B** completely   **C** accurately   **D** entirely
2 **A** fresh   **B** initial   **C** early   **D** young
3 **A** ranging   **B** continuing   **C** expanding   **D** covering
4 **A** take on   **B** come to   **C** go over   **D** make up
5 **A** consume   **B** feed   **C** eat   **D** absorb
6 **A** whereas   **B** nevertheless   **C** while   **D** though
7 **A** recognised   **B** distinguished   **C** noticed   **D** specified
8 **A** maintain   **B** follow   **C** remain   **D** hold

Listening Part 1

Read the question carefully to make sure you understand which speaker the question is referring to.

Exam advice

13 **You will hear people talking in eight different situations. For questions 1–8, choose the best answer (A, B or C).**

1 You hear a man speaking to his friend about a neighbour's pet bird. What does the man say about it?
   A It whistles whenever it's happy.
   B It doesn't like to be kept inside its cage.
   C It helps his neighbour to feel less lonely.

2 You hear a mother talking to her son about an incident at the beach. What is the mother doing?
   A forbidding her son from going to the beach at certain times
   B advising her son to go in the sea only with other people
   C suggesting that her son is exaggerating what happened

3 You hear a man talking to his friend about a dog walking service. What does the man say about it?
   A It's reassuring that his dog is being cared for.
   B It's more economical than he expected it to be.
   C It's conveniently located for his place of work.

4 You hear two friends talking about their exam results. How do they both feel?
   A relieved to have finally finished
   B satisfied with their performance
   C surprised about a particular mark

5 You overhear a father and daughter talking on a train. Why did the father want to catch the train?
   A to enjoy the beautiful scenery
   B to have a relaxing journey
   C to save money on travel

6 You hear a woman talking on a radio programme about personal challenges. What is the woman talking about?
   A a job interview
   B a driving test
   C a music exam

7 You hear a blind man talking about his guide dog, Lola. What is the man doing?

   A justifying getting rid of his dog when she retires

   B explaining why he will have more than one

   C admitting that he would like to have a new dog

8 You hear a man talking to an employee of a cruise company. What is the man refusing to do?

   A allow a name to be changed

   B use his own computer

   C pay an additional fee

Writing Part 2

An email

1 Read the Writing Part 2 exam question and the model answer.

> You have received an email from your English-speaking friend Jonathan.
>
> From: **Jonathan**
> Subject: **Pets**
>
> Fantastic news! My parents are thinking about letting me have a pet at last!
> Do you think it's a good idea to get a pet? If so, what kind of animal? I'll need some good reasons to give my parents. If you don't think it's a good idea, let me know why not.
> Tell me what you think. See you soon,
> Jonathan
>
> Write your **email** in **140–190** words in an appropriate style.

Hi Jonathan,

What fantastic news that you're finally allowed to get a pet. I think it's a brilliant idea, because pets are great companions. Getting a dog would be amazing. They're fun to play with and they're very loyal friends, but you'd have to take it for a walk every day, even when it's raining. Another idea is a cat. They're easier to look after than dogs because you don't need to take them for walks or give them as much attention. They don't play with you a lot, but they sit on your lap and keep you company. I don't think you should get a pet that doesn't do much, like a fish or a bird. You still have to feed it and clean its bowl or cage, but after a while it'd get quite boring. So, overall, I think you should get a dog. You can tell your parents that taking it for walks will be good exercise for you and that looking after it will teach you how to be responsible, too. But remember, it's a big commitment – you might have your pet for a long time. Let me know what you decide.

Write soon,

Chiara

> Always make a plan and underline the key parts of the email that you have to deal with.
>
> **Exam advice**

2 Tick (✓) the points in Jonathan's email that Chiara answers. Write notes on what she says.

   1 Do you think it's a good idea to get a pet?

   2 If so, what kind of animal?

   3 Reasons to give his parents.

   4 Why it might be a bad idea.

3 Put a bracket ([ ) where you think the paragraphs should begin in Chiara's email.

4 Is the email within the word count of 140–190 words? Is there a greeting at the beginning and a sign-off at the end?

5 Match the informal expressions (1–8) with the formal expressions (A–H).

   1 Dear Mark / Hi Mark / Hello Mark ....

   2 Great to hear from you / Thanks for your email ....

   3 Sorry for taking so long to get back to you ....

   4 How's it going? / How are you? ....

   5 You asked me about ....

   6 You really must / Why don't you ....

   7 Here's ....

   8 Write soon ....

   A In answer to your first question

   B Dear Mr Smith

   C Please find attached

   D Thank you for your email

   E May I suggest / I recommend

   F I look forward to hearing from you

   G I apologise for my late reply

   H I hope this email finds you well

13 House space

Grammar

Causative *have* and *get*

1a Look at Picture 1. What does Jennifer need to have done to the room? Complete the sentences with the correct form of the verbs in the box.

> carpet   clean   deliver   fix   hang   ~~paint~~

1 She wants *to have/get* the walls *painted* .
2 She needs .... the floor ....
3 She'd like .... the windows ....
4 She has to .... the light ....
5 She wants .... some pictures ....
6 She is going .... some furniture ....

1b Look at Picture 2. What has Jennifer had done and what hasn't she had done?

1 *She has had/got the walls painted.*
2 ....
3 ....
4 ....
5 ....
6 ....

Expressing obligation and permission

2 Choose the correct option in *italics*.

1 *I don't let my children / My children don't have to* answer the front door. They have to tell me if they hear the doorbell ring.

2 You *don't have to / mustn't* wash the dishes in the sink. We've got a dishwasher.

3 I *did need to plant / needn't have planted* so many tomatoes in the garden. They're so cheap at the supermarket this year.

4 We *are not supposed to / are allowed to* have parties in our flat, but we invite all the neighbours so nobody complains.

5 You *couldn't / shouldn't* have put the recycling out tonight. It doesn't get collected till Thursday.

6 We *wouldn't let us / weren't allowed to* build another floor on our house. It was opposed by our neighbours, who said it would block their view of the park.

7 We *needn't / can't* park our car in front of our flat – there are double yellow lines on the street.

8 I think we *should / are allowed to* hang pictures on the walls of our rented apartment, as long as we fill in the holes before we move out.

1

2

Vocabulary

Describing where you live

 1 Complete the text with the words in the box.

> amenities   balcony   central   en-suite
> links   neighbours   open-plan
> outside   peaceful   residential

We've just moved to a new house in a nice, quiet,
(1) .... area. I used to like living in the
city centre as it was such a **(2)** ....
location and I got on really well with my
(3) .... But it had become too small for
us all, with only one bathroom and no
(4) .... area for the kids to play in. It was
very noisy as well, because of all the traffic. Our
new house is much more **(5)** .... and we
have a lot more space. There's an **(6)** ....
bathroom in all the bedrooms and there's a huge
(7) .... living area. There's the garden,
too, which is so much better for us than the tiny
(8) .... we had in the old flat. It's not
as close to the transport **(9)** .... , but
there are lots of local **(10)** .... , such as a
swimming pool and a shopping centre.

space, place, room, area, location and *square*

 2 Choose the correct option in *italics*.

1 They have barbecues in the picnic *space / area*
   of our local park.
2 I need to get a new car with more leg
   place / room in the back. My kids are
   quite tall now.
3 I've been driving around for twenty minutes
   but I can't find a parking *space / square*.
4 I need to find a good hiding *location / place*
   for the front door key. What about under this
   plant pot?
5 Our new house is in the perfect *location / space*.
   It's close to schools, parks and transport links.
6 Every Saturday in our town there's an outdoor
   market in the main *square / place*.
7 Where do you suggest as a meeting
   place / room? Outside the bus station?
8 We just don't have enough floor *space / place* to
   have two beds in this room.

Listening Part 2

 You may need to write up to three
words, but usually the answer is only
one or two, or a number. **Exam advice**

14 You will hear a woman called Julie Marshall talking about her
work as an estate agent selling houses and other properties.
For questions 1–10, complete the sentences with a word or
short phrase.

Selling houses for a living

It was Julie's **(1)** .... who encouraged her to become an
estate agent.

Julie was first attracted to her job by the **(2)** ....
on offer.

Julie was given a **(3)** .... when she completed
her studies.

Julie believes that **(4)** .... is the most important quality
in an estate agent.

Julie has to ask home buyers about their **(5)** .... when
arranging viewings.

The most common question that potential buyers ask Julie is
about the **(6)** .... of the house.

Julie says that **(7)** .... is vital when showing people
around a house.

Julie mentions an issue with the **(8)** .... after selling a
couple a city centre flat.

Julie once sold a property for **(9)** .... pounds, the
biggest sale in the company's history.

Julie finds having discussions with **(10)** .... the most
challenging part of the job.

Writing Part 2
An article

Exam advice

Try to use linking words and phrases to make sure that your answer flows well and is easy to follow.

 1 Read the Writing Part 2 exam question and the model answer. Then put a tick (✓) next to the recommendations for writing an article that have been included in the model answer.

1 It should have a catchy, interesting title.
2 It is a good idea to include a question.
3 It should be written in paragraphs.
4 It needs to answer all the points in the question.
5 It should make comments or give opinions.
6 It must be between 140 and 190 words.

You have seen this announcement on a website:

Articles wanted!

My dream home

Tell us about your dream home.

Where would it be? What would it look like?

Write an article answering these questions. We will publish the best articles next week.

Write your **article** in **140–190** words.

My dream home

My dream home would be a cottage by the sea. It would be somewhere green and pretty like Ireland. It would be a short walk from a sandy beach, but not somewhere where there are too many people. I love getting away from crazy city life, so I think this house would make me feel peaceful and relaxed. Who wouldn't love to live near a beach?

It would be an old-fashioned house on two floors, with bedrooms upstairs and the living area downstairs. I would paint the front door red and there would be a colourful flower garden in front of the house. The living area would have a big, comfortable sofa with an open fire for the winter evenings, and the kitchen would be large enough for cooking all the food I would grow in the garden during the summer.

Sadly, I don't think I will ever live in my dream home as my job as an engineer will always keep me in the city. My dream house is certainly very different from the noisy city flat I live in now!

2 Match the types of detail (A–E) with the examples from the article (1–5).

Type of detail
A providing a description ....
B making a comparison ....
C giving an opinion ....
D adding an example ....
E describing feelings ....

Example
1 I love getting away from crazy city life, so I think this house would make me feel peaceful and relaxed.
2 Sadly, I don't think I will ever live in my dream home as my job as an engineer will always keep me in the city.
3 My dream house is certainly very different from the noisy city flat I live in now!
4 I would paint the front door red and there would be a colourful flower garden in front of the house.
5 It would be somewhere green and pretty like Ireland.

Reading and Use of English Part 5

Exam advice

An option may seem right when you read the question, but find evidence for it in the text before you mark it as correct.

You are going to read an article written by an architect with predictions for the houses of the future. For questions 1–6, choose the answer (A, B, C or D) which you think fits best according to the text.

1 In the first paragraph, what does the writer imply about the homes of the future?
A They will be more solid and secure.
B They are going to be difficult to build.
C People's views of them are often misguided.
D People are likely to be more reliant on home technology.

2 According to the writer, the homeowners of the future will be most concerned about
A spending too much money building their house.
B reducing their energy consumption.
C having a large enough garden.
D increasing the value of their property.

3 What does *restricted* mean in line 24?
A closed
B inadequate
C controlled
D limited

4 What does the writer see as the most significant role of plants in the houses of the future?
A to improve the homeowner's health
B to keep the house warm
C to be decorative
D to provide nutrition

5 What does *them* refer to in line 54?

   A local councils

   B rainwater collection tanks

   C laws

   D fines

6 What is the writer doing in the final paragraph?

   A arguing that we're much closer to having sustainable housing than many people think

   B questioning whether sustainable housing will help prevent environmental damage

   C admitting that sustainable housing is possible only for wealthy people

   D pointing out that a lot more research into sustainable housing needs to be done

The homes of the future

If you ask most people what the homes of the future will be like, they will probably mention robots cleaning the floors and smart thermostats that can learn a person's heating needs and adjust the temperature accordingly. The real direction that housing is likely to take, though, is not towards trendy gadgets, entertainment and things that make our lives more comfortable but rather towards safeguarding our future existence. Homes will be built as complex, artificial ecosystems, allowing a closer connection between humans and the natural world.

Of course, it would be naive to think that home buyers will be willing to pay the high costs of the building materials needed to make their houses sustainable and eco-friendly. The bottom line will always be an issue for people – meaning that keeping costs low is a key factor. On the other hand, people are becoming a lot more conscious of how an initial investment can result in long-term benefit. They understand that an eco-friendly house will lead to lower energy costs, which will save them cash in the long run. In reality, the environmentally-friendly qualities of a property will be the main priority for the next generation of homeowners.

Size is also turning into a significant factor when designing houses. The rapid growth in population means that there are fewer areas available to build on. As a result, the houses of the

24 future will need to be built in more **restricted** spaces, especially in urban areas. But this doesn't necessarily mean a lack of room inside the new properties. One solution is to construct narrower buildings, with more floors. Houses like this can be easily built using a limited number of large prefabricated pieces; these are made elsewhere and then assembled on site. The pieces lock together tightly, making the houses airtight, which has the added bonus of reducing heat loss.

It's not just the type of building materials that we use which will change in the coming years, though. Biophilic design, which is the architectural term for buildings which incorporate greater access to nature, will play an important part in transforming the houses of the future. No one can deny the visual benefits of making dull urban places green, but plants have other useful functions as well. Studies have found that being surrounded by plant life has enormous positive psychological effects on the homeowner. The fact that these buildings lower stress,

and enhance mood and productivity is reason enough to encourage this type of design. Additionally, having plants on the walls and roofs of your house could provide valuable insulation, as well as a source of food. The possibilities, it's fair to say, are endless.

With all this greenery, access to water is going to become even more important. Gone will be the days of rooftop pipes sending rainwater into public drainage systems. Rainwater will become valuable, and will be used to keep gardens alive as well as for non-drinking purposes, such as in bathrooms and for washing machines. Many cities have passed laws making it mandatory for rainwater collection tanks to be part of all future homes, with some local councils even imposing fines for those who don't adhere to **them**. 54

Some critics still think that sustainable architecture is a distant dream, one that will only ever be achievable for those with money. They also consider that the overall benefit to the environment will be minimal. However, apart from the fact that we should be celebrating any small steps that minimise the negative environmental impact of buildings, the progress towards eco-friendly housing is gaining pace. Sooner rather than later sustainable housing will be a reality for everyone.

14 Fiesta!

The passive

1 Complete the newspaper article with the passive form of the verbs in brackets.

The Strawberry Fair

A celebration of the start of strawberry season **(1)** .... (hold) in the village of Linleyside since the middle of the 19th century. Linleyside **(2)** .... (surround) by strawberry farms these days, but the first **(3)** .... (set up) in 1850, when a huge glass greenhouse **(4)** .... (build) by a local landowning family called the Greysons, so that strawberries could **(5)** .... (cultivate) and then sold in London. It was a great help to the economy of the village because the strawberries in the greenhouse **(6)** .... (grow) and picked

by local people who **(7)** .... (employ) by the Greyson family. The traditional May Day celebrations became the Strawberry Fair, which **(8)** .... (still hold) today during the first week of May.

In the 19th century, pink and red clothes **(9)** .... (wear) by the pickers so that the strawberry stains **(10)** .... (hide), and the same colours **(11)** .... (still wear) at the festival today. Over the last thirty years, the fair has grown from being a local celebration to a festival that **(12)** .... (attend) by thousands of people. Strawberry cakes, jams and biscuits **(13)** .... (sell), and fairgoers

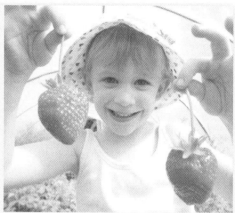

eat kilos of strawberries. They **(14)** .... (also crush) to make juice. If you decide to go to this year's festival, why not stay at the Greysons' stately home, which **(15)** .... (now convert) into a hotel?

The passive with reporting verbs

2 Rewrite the newspaper headlines using the verbs in brackets. You will need to add extra words to each sentence.

1
> CURE FOR THE COMMON COLD DISCOVERED

It has been reported that a cure for the common cold has been discovered. .... (report)

2
> ESCAPED PRISONER STILL IN THE AREA

.... (believe)

3
> UNEMPLOYMENT TO FALL NEXT YEAR

.... (expect)

4
> STORMS WILL PROBABLY HIT COAST ON SUNDAY

.... (think)

5
> MARIA CALLAS IS MOST POPULAR OPERA SINGER EVER

.... (consider)

6
> MAN MISSING FOR 10 YEARS FOUND ON DESERT ISLAND

.... (confirm)

Vocabulary

Describing festivals and celebrations

1 **Complete the sentences with the verbs in the box.**

> celebrate   commemorate   dress up   gather round
> hold   let off   march   play   perform   wear

1 Last year for his birthday party, each guest had to
.... as a famous historical person and
.... clothes from the time he or she had lived in.
2 When Americans .... Thanksgiving, it is to
.... a harvest feast that settlers had in 1621.
3 At the Autumn Festival in my town, the local children
.... from school into the town square and then
.... a big statue to sing songs together.
4 At New Year, New Yorkers .... a street party in
Times Square and .... fireworks at midnight.
5 Both my children are involved in the Arts Festival this
year. My son is going to .... in a musical and my
daughter will .... the violin in the orchestra.

Suffixes

2 **Add suffixes to the words to make nouns for people, then
underline the different word in each group.**

1 motor ....   tour ....
  economy ....   refuge ....

2 research ....   collect ....
  survive ....   investigate ....

3 consult ....   conduct ....
  assist ....   contest ....

4 sales ....   sports ....
  business ....   manage ....

5 special ....   novel ....
  comedy ....   pharmacy ....

6 wait ....   sail ....
  farm ....   mine ....

Listening Part 4

Don't get stuck on one question if it's
difficult. Move on to the next question.
You will be able to go back to difficult
questions the second time you listen.

Exam advice

15 **You will hear an interview with Margaret Blake, a
teacher who organises a poetry festival for young
people. For questions 1–7, choose the best answer
(A, B or C).**

1 What surprised Margaret the most about her
group of students?
A They were writing poetry for the internet.
B They were performing their poetry in person.
C They were sharing their poetry anonymously.

2 Margaret started the poetry festival because
A she was asked to by her students.
B she hoped to get other people interested
in poetry.
C she wanted to find other young poets.

3 How did Margaret feel about the response she got?
A grateful that so many young poets wanted
to take part
B amazed that a lot of the young poets
lived nearby
C pleased that several young poets wanted
to help her

4 What made Margaret realise that the first festival
was going to be special?
A the media attention the event received
B the distances that were travelled
C the appreciative audiences

5 When talking about the future of the festival,
Margaret suggests that she would like to
A expand it to other types of writing.
B have larger locations for the performances.
C make it longer to include more poets.

6 Margaret says that a book of poems from this
year's festival
A has just become available.
B can be downloaded from the website.
C has already sold out.

7 What does Margaret say about the students that
first inspired the festival?
A They are all helping her now.
B They are too old to participate.
C They no longer read poetry aloud
to each other.

You are going to read a magazine article in which the writer talks about the Venice Carnival. Six sentences have been removed from the article. Choose from the sentences A–G the one which fits each gap (1–6). There is one sentence which you do not need to use.

Once you have decided on an option, cross it off the list so you don't waste time reading it again.

Exam advice

The Venice Carnival

I love Italy and I think Venice is the most romantic city in Europe. One day I was checking flight offers online and saw that tickets to Venice for the next weekend were only about 15 euros return. I couldn't believe it, as the Venice Carnival was on as well. I quickly bought one for myself and one for my friend Sophie because I knew she loved Venice, too.

The next Friday we got on the plane and in just over two hours we were there. We went to a place called Mestre by bus, where we had booked our hotel. This is a good tip for any traveller because hotels in Venice can be extremely expensive. **1** [ ] We saw that Mestre, which is just over ten minutes away from Venice by train, was a much cheaper option and we found a hotel at a very good price. Because we had arrived in the morning, it would have been easier just to go straight to Venice for the day, but we needed to check into the hotel to change into our costumes. **2** [ ] We put them on, did a bit of a spin and walked to the train station. It felt a bit strange being in the street in our fancy dress.

When we got to Santa Lucia station on the train from Mestre, we hopped onto a *vaporetto*, a kind of small ferry. Taking a boat on the Grand Canal was amazing and I took lots of pictures. When we got off the *vaporetto*, we walked through the small streets, crossing squares and bridges. We

needed to add the final touch to our costumes, so we were looking for a shop to buy our masks. **3** [ ] We tried on a lot of very beautiful designs – some of them cost as much as 300 euros, but we settled on two that looked really effective and covered only half our faces. The shop assistant spoke to us in Italian. **4** [ ]

Surprisingly, there didn't seem to be many people in costume, so a lot of people took photos of us as we walked through the streets. **5** [ ] As it was the opening day of the Carnival, we were extremely excited. When we got to St Mark's Square, there were a lot more people dressed like us – in fact, it was absolutely packed. The opening of the Carnival was quite impressive. Different teams raced across the main canal on gondolas, the traditional Venetian boats. All the teams were in costume. **6** [ ] They all looked very colourful and original. In the square, the first of the costume competitions began, and we were also surrounded by magicians, acrobats and lots of other performers. In the evening, as it got dark, music and dancing began in the square. I really think going to the Venice Carnival in costume helps you get into the spirit of the festival and adds to the fun. Rather than just watching the Carnival, we became a part of it.

A We laughed so much – it was like they thought we were famous or something.	**E** Sophie and I had hired them at home to wear to the Carnival.
B If you are like me, a normal student with not a lot of cash, you need to be smart about where you stay.	**F** It didn't have a very elaborate design but it was elegant.
C There were some in black with rich decorations, others were all in pink and some were even dressed like pandas.	**G** It didn't take us long to find one – they were selling them almost everywhere.
D She was surprised when we told her we were two English girls and congratulated us on our costumes.	

Reading and Use of English Part 3

Always check that the word you have chosen fits the context and is spelt correctly.

Exam advice

For questions 1–8, read the text below. Use the word given in capitals at the end of some of the lines to form a word that fits in the gap in the same line. There is an example at the beginning (0).

The Cannes Film Festival

Every spring the biggest names in the film industry arrive on the **(0)** glamorous French Riviera for the Cannes Film Festival. First held in the autumn of 1946, the festival was moved to the spring to avoid direct **(1)** .... with the Venice Film Festival. Films are shown at the Palais des Festivals et des Congrès, and the festival awards prizes to **(2)** .... films from all over the globe.

For ten days, huge crowds of onlookers and photographers gather to witness the world's most **(3)** .... actors and directors arriving on the red carpet to promote their films. The festival's board of directors appoints juries, who have the sole **(4)** .... for selecting the winning films on the basis of their **(5)** .... merit. The Palme d'Or is awarded **(6)** .... to the best film and is the most prestigious award at the festival. As well as recognising the many **(7)** .... of talented actors and directors, it is also where people in the film industry can **(8)** .... ideas and plan future productions.

GLAMOUR

COMPETE

INNOVATE

FASHION

RESPONSE

ART
ANNUAL

ACHIEVE

CHANGE

Writing Part 1

An essay

Remember to write more or less the right number of words. If you write too much you may include information which is not relevant.

Exam advice

Read the Writing Part 1 exam question and the model answer.

In your English class you have been discussing festivals. Now your English teacher has asked you to write an essay. Write an **essay** in **140–190** words using all the notes and giving reasons for your point of view.

Some people believe that music festivals have a negative impact on the local community. Do you agree?

Notes
Write about:
1. the environment
2. local businesses
3. .... (your own idea)

(1) .... Though they can be very disruptive, they are usually on for only a few days a year and bring great financial advantages.

(2) .... Visitors camping on site produce a large amount of rubbish. Noise pollution is also an issue, not only from the loud music, but also from people shouting and clapping. Some community members do not feel safe with so many strangers in the area and may even choose to move away while the festival is on.

(3) .... People go into the town and purchase food. They fill the hotels and restaurants and buy petrol for their cars. All these factors help to enrich the local economy.

(4) .... Once the mess left by festival-goers is cleaned up and the noise has stopped, the negative impact of a festival is over quite quickly, but the benefits are long-lasting.

Match the topic sentences (A–D) with the correct essay paragraph (1–4).

A Music festivals have the advantage of bringing a great deal of money to nearby businesses. ....

B Festivals can cause a lot of nuisance to the local community. ....

C Overall, I believe the financial benefits of a music festival outweigh any disadvantages. ....

D The effect that a music festival has on a local community can be both negative and positive. ....

Workbook answer key with audioscripts Units 1–14

Unit 1 A family affair

Grammar

Present perfect simple and continuous

1
1 haven't been
2 have/'ve been organising
3 have/'ve changed
4 have/'ve been staying
5 have/'ve been sleeping
6 has/'s been helping
7 have/'ve loved
8 have/'ve found
9 have been
10 have/'ve spent
11 have/'ve been going /'ve been
12 have/'ve seen
13 have/'ve decided
14 have/'ve (already) spent
15 have/'ve looked

2
1 Have you found an apartment yet?
2 Have you visited the Statue of Liberty?
3 Have you been eating healthily?
4 What Broadway shows have you seen?
5 Have you been taking the subway everywhere?

3
1 No, I haven't.   **2** Yes, I have.   **3** No, I haven't.
4 (I have/'ve seen) *The Lion King*.   **5** Yes, I have.

Vocabulary

Phrasal verbs

1
1 C   **2** F   **3** B   **4** D   **5** E   **6** A

2
1 turn (the information) into   **2** turn up   **3** made up
4 hang out   **5** carry on   **6** count on

Collocations with *make* and *do*

3
1 do   **2** make   **3** did   **4** make   **5** make
6 did   **7** made   **8** make   **9** done   **10** make

Listening Part 1

1 C   **2** B   **3** B   **4** A   **5** C   **6** C   **7** A   **8** A

Track 2

Narrator: One. You hear a young man talking about his friend's new haircut.

Man: My best friend recently dyed her hair pink. Not just a few light pink highlights, but a hot pink – the kind of thing that people stare at in the street. It does look striking and it rather suits her, but I thought she was crazy getting it done, as we've both just graduated and have been looking for jobs. <u>It's really taking a chance having such a loud hairstyle if you want someone to hire you</u>, but she's just got a fantastic job working for a fashion magazine. She told me she thought her hair was why she got the job – it made her stand out. I don't know about that, though.

Narrator: Two. You hear a man talking to his daughter about meeting her mother for the first time.

Daughter: Dad, how did you first meet Mum?

Father: We went to university together. One day I needed a book for an assignment. There was just one copy left in the library, but before I could get to it this girl reached up and grabbed it off the shelf.

Daughter: So you read the book together, then?

Father: No, actually she'd already read it. She'd used her university identity card as a bookmark and had left it inside. She laughed when she shook the book and the card fell out. <u>I realised then that she hadn't meant to be rude – she told me later that she was worried about losing her card. I think I'd have felt the same.</u>

Narrator: Three. You hear a girl talking about getting driving lessons from her father.

Girl: When I turned 17, I was really keen to get my driving licence, but lessons were so expensive. So my dad offered to teach me in his car. <u>I was a bit hesitant at first because I remembered my mum had said that when he taught her to drive years ago, he'd got really annoyed with her because she took so long to learn.</u> But that wasn't the case. Even when I slammed on the brakes or took a corner a bit too fast, he kept his cool. He actually taught me so well, I passed the test first time.

Narrator: Four. You overhear a man and a woman talking about a new café.

Man: I went to that new café on the corner yesterday for lunch.

Woman: It's nice to have a local café again, isn't it?

Man: I thought so too, but it was so crowded! I couldn't get a table and just ordering a sandwich to take to the park took twenty minutes.

Woman: I was there on Tuesday and I had no problems getting served or finding a seat. Oh well. <u>It's good for business if it's popular. The one there before was always empty – that's why it closed down.</u>

Man: You certainly can't keep a place like that open if nobody actually goes there. I think I was practically the only customer in the old place.

Narrator: Five. You hear a woman talking about a tree in her neighbour's garden.

Woman: My next-door neighbour has a huge tree growing in his garden and one of the branches was pressing up against my bedroom window. I asked him to cut the branch down, which he did yesterday, but now it's lying on the grass in my garden and I can't get in touch with him. <u>What do you reckon I should do?</u> I certainly don't want to get into an argument with a neighbour, but I have a feeling he thinks it's up to me to get rid of it. It's enormous, so there's no way I can manage it by myself. I hope he calls me soon.

Narrator: Six. You hear a husband and wife planning a holiday.

Man: Let's go to Greece again this summer. We had such a good time there last year.

Woman: As a matter of fact, I was thinking we could go somewhere more exotic this year.

Man: Really? But you said it was the most memorable holiday you'd ever had.

Woman: Sure I did. But I get hardly any time off and I really want to make the most of it. We can't just keep going back to the same place. I've never been to Asia, for instance.

Man: <u>OK, fine – on the condition that we go somewhere with a beach.</u> I don't feel like I've had a holiday unless I've spent some time away from the city.

Narrator: Seven. You hear two friends talking about a photograph.

Boy: Who's this in the photo here?

Girl: It's a picture of my grandmother when she was a teenager.

Boy: It's a great photo.

Girl: Yeah, it is, isn't it? I didn't know her when she was that age, of course, but the photo tells me she's been the same type of person all her life. She looks so cheerful and full of energy. <u>It'd be great to go through life just as she has – she's always seen the good side of everything</u>, despite any difficulties she's had. Of course, she looks different now – she's elderly – but I instantly recognise the woman I know in this photograph.

Reading and Use of English Part 2

1 such	**2** of	**3** the	**4** to
5 with	**6** been	**7** by	**8** if / though / when

Writing

My sisters and I

I am so glad ~~Im~~ **I'm** not an only child. Of course, my parents are ~~grate~~ **great**, but they don't always understand the problems of being young. ~~Thats~~ **That's** when I ~~appreciete~~ **appreciate** having sisters. I'm in the middle of two sisters and we spend all our time together. They are my best friends and we get on really well. Of ~~corse~~, **course**, we sometimes fight – for example, if I borrow a sister's ~~cloths~~ **clothes** without ~~permision~~ **permission** or if our bedroom gets ~~to~~ **too** messy. They are much ~~tidyer~~ **tidier** than me. We ~~do'nt~~ **don't** usually have many problems but if I argue ~~whit~~ **with** one sister, there is always the other one to talk to? **.** We have the same ~~taist~~ **taste** in music, too. I think that without my ~~sisters'~~ **sisters**, life would be very boring. ~~would~~ **Would** I like to have a brother, too? I'm not so sure. I think I like having sisters more.

Unit 2 Leisure and pleasure

Grammar

Making comparisons

1

1 much hotter	**5** much
2 much more difficult	**6** far
3 more, a better	**7** much faster, more easily
4 more	**8** as good as

2

1 as relaxing as / more relaxing than	**5** even faster
2 correct	**6** less complicated than
3 as expensive as	**7** (much) more enjoyable than
4 correct	**8** correct

Adjectives with -ed and -ing

3

1 boring	**2** astonished	**3** worried	**4** puzzled
5 motivating	**6** irritated	**7** exhausting	**8** excited

4

Adjective	Verb	Noun
bored/boring	to bore	boredom
confuse/confusing	to confuse	confusion
embarrassed/embarrassing	to embarrass	embarrassment
excited/exciting	to excite	excitement
exhausted/exhausting	to exhaust	exhaustion
irritated/irritating	to irritate	irritation
motivated/motivating	to motivate	motivation
worried/worrying	to worry	worry

Vocabulary

Phrasal verbs

1

1 G	**2** H	**3** E	**4** A	**5** B	**6** C	**7** F	**8** D

2

1 ended up	**2** came across	**3** thrown herself into	**4** count on
5 went on	**6** came along	**7** ran out of	**8** came up against

Listening Part 2

1 hobby	**2** cool	**3** street	**4** space
5 bookshop	**6** pottery	**7** (good) (video) camera	**8** 100,000
9 (very) wealthy	**10** (TV) (production) company		

The problem with a business like this is that I no longer have any time for anything but work. There's always something to do – like picking up furniture that someone has phoned me about. When your passion becomes your job, it's difficult to know when you're working and when you're relaxing. Perhaps that's a good thing. I really love what I do and I'm actually now quite famous. I'm never going to be <u>very wealthy</u>, but I do get a lot of views on my channel, which is starting to bring in extra income to add to the money I get from the furniture sales. Recently, I was approached by a <u>production company</u> about appearing in some sort of restoration and design programme. And a talent agent wants to represent me. I'm going to film the first episode in the summer and see if any TV networks are interested in it. I'm feeling very positive about my future.

Reading and Use of English Part 5

1 D **2** B **3** A **4** C **5** C **6** B

Reading and Use of English Part 4

1 asked me to buy (her) OR asked (me) if I would/could/'d buy (her)
2 taste nearly as good
3 run out of milk so
4 as much money as me
5 it hadn't been for
6 didn't/did not mean to break

Writing Part 2 (An article)

1
1 Each week we go to a different place **because** we like to vary the landscapes we paint.
2 I enjoy the company of the other artists **and** I create some lovely paintings, too.
3 I would suggest it to others **because** it's a good opportunity to experience the natural environment.
4 I didn't have much experience **but** the teacher taught me how to use colours and draw the outlines.
5 I saw a poster advertising landscape painting lessons **and** I decided to enrol on the course.
6 I would never give it up **because** I have made so many new friends and it helps me to be creative.
7 I really love spending time outside **but** if it's raining, we paint in the studio.

2
A 5 **B** 4 1 **C** 7 2 **D** 3 6

Suggested order of the text:
I saw a poster advertising landscape painting lessons and I decided to enrol on the course.
I didn't have much experience but the teacher taught me how to use colours and draw the outlines. Each week we go to a different place because we like to vary the landscapes we paint.
I really love spending time outside but if it's raining, we paint in the studio. I enjoy the company of the other artists and I create some lovely paintings, too.
I would suggest it to others because it's a good opportunity to experience the natural environment. I would never give it up because I have made so many new friends and it helps me to be creative.

Unit 3 Happy holidays?

Grammar
Past simple, past continuous, past perfect simple and past perfect continuous

1
1 went   **2** knew   **3** woke up   **4** was raining
5 decided   **6** hoped   **7** heard   **8** was listening
9 stopped   **10** was parking   **11** was getting   **12** arrived
13 were looking forward to   **14** set off

2
1 had been driving   **2** had already taken off   **3** hadn't travelled
4 had forgotten   **5** hadn't been doing   **6** had already paid

3
1 decided   **2** had been working   **3** realised
4 had packed   **5** had sailed   **6** hadn't brought
7 hadn't taken   **8** felt   **9** hadn't planned
10 found   **11** was getting   **12** bought

at, *in* and *on* in time phrases

4
1 at   **2** in   **3** on   **4** in   **5** on   **6** at

Vocabulary
Travel words

1

Across	**1** business	**3** overnight	**6** travel	**7** way
	8 trip	**10** holiday	**12** weekend	
Down	**2** sightseeing	**4** village	**5** agent	
	9 journey	**11** abroad		

Suffixes

2
1 colourful   **2** reasonable   **3** successful   **4** energetic
5 natural   **6** adventurous   **7** doubtful   **8** thrilling
9 accessible   **10** crowded   **11** mysterious   **12** friendly

Listening Part 3

1 G   **2** C   **3** H   **4** A   **5** E

Track 4

Narrator: Speaker 1
Speaker 1: It was the first day of our holiday in Spain. I'd taken the family down to the beach to the umbrellas and chairs we'd rented for the whole week. We couldn't have had a better position, right up the front and almost at the water's edge. I was just settling into my chair when someone greeted me by name. <u>I looked across and who was it but my next door neighbour!</u> Not only was his beach chair and umbrella right next to ours, but he was also staying at the same hotel! He didn't seem that surprised but I was speechless. It's a small world.

Narrator: Speaker 2
Speaker 2: I was on holiday in Venice with a friend and we were doing a tour of a four-hundred-year-old palace where the ceilings were covered in amazing paintings. My friend suddenly burst out laughing and started photographing something in the corner of one of the rooms. I asked her what was going on, but before she could tell me I'd spotted it myself. A chubby little cherub in the painting was peering over the edge of a cloud <u>and its face looked exactly like mine – I couldn't believe it!</u> I still have a photo and people I know always look out for it when they go to Venice.

Narrator: Speaker 3

Speaker 3: I was coming back from a holiday in the USA after a really tiring rock-climbing tour. My flight was going from Dallas to London – and I wasn't looking forward to the ten-hour trip. As I was checking in, I was told there were too many people booked in on the flight and would I take a plane the next day instead. <u>This really wasn't part of my plan, but I agreed,</u> and the airline put me up in a very nice hotel overnight. When I checked in the next day, they told me I'd been upgraded to Business Class. I'd suspected this might happen as I'd done the airline a favour.

Narrator: Speaker 4

Speaker 4: I've always been very active in the conservation movement, and I love helping to record where and when particular birds are seen. I recently went on holiday to Scotland in the hope of tracking down one species of bird people feared had died out. <u>I can still hardly believe it, but when I was in the garden of the hotel, I suddenly saw one sitting on a branch above my head.</u> By the time I'd raced up to my room and come back ready with my camera, it was nowhere to be seen. It was fantastic to discover it hasn't become extinct, even if I don't have proof of that.

Narrator: Speaker 5

Speaker 5: I was walking along the beach on holiday in Nova Scotia in Canada when I nearly tripped over something sticking out of the sand between the rocks. On closer inspection, I saw it was an old bottle sealed with a cork. I got it open at the hotel and pulled out a rolled-up piece of paper with nothing on it but a name and address to contact, which I did when I got back home. Amazingly, the person was still living at the same address. The bottle had been put in the water by a schoolboy in Cornwall 30 years before as a science experiment. <u>He was now grown up and could hardly believe it when I got in touch.</u>

Writing Part 2 (A report)

1 The purpose of　**2** In terms of　**3** It is also a benefit　**4** Disadvantages
5 In addition　**6** I would highly recommend　**7** Although

Reading and Use of English Part 7

1 B　**2** D　**3** B　**4** C　**5** A　**6** D　**7** B　**8** C　**9** D　**10** A

Unit 4 Food, glorious food

Grammar

so and *such*, *too* and *enough*

1
1 enough　**2** enough　**3** too　**4** such　**5** so little
6 so few　**7** such a　**8** sweet enough　**9** too　**10** so many

2
1 ~~much~~ many　　　　　　**5** correct
2 correct　　　　　　　　　**6** correct
3 ~~too much~~ so much　　　**7** ~~such expensive~~ so expensive
4 ~~there is enough~~ there are enough　**8** correct

Vocabulary

Food and diet

1
1 diet　**2** dish　**3** meal　**4** dish　**5** organic
6 food　**7** filling　**8** fresh　**9** meals　**10** simple

2
Across　**4** convenience　**5** tasty　**6** recipe
Down　**1** balanced　**2** lifestyle　**3** nutrition　**4** catering　**6** raw

Reading and Use of English Part 1

1 C　**2** A　**3** A　**4** D　**5** C　**6** C　**7** B　**8** D

Reading and Use of English Part 6

1 D　**2** C　**3** B　**4** F　**5** A　**6** G

Listening Part 4

1 A　**2** B　**3** C　**4** B　**5** A　**6** B　**7** C

Track 5

Narrator: You will hear a radio interview with a man called Mike Jones, who has recently been a contestant on a TV cooking show. For questions 1 to 7, choose the best answer (A, B or C).

Interviewer: I have here in the studio Mike Jones, who's recently been a contestant on the TV cooking show *Stars of the Kitchen*. How did you get on the show, Mike?

Mike: <u>Well, it was completely unexpected as it was my sister who entered me into the competition.</u> She likes my cooking and thought I'd be a good contestant. When the production company phoned me, I thought it was a joke. It wasn't something I'd ever considered doing as I'm normally quite introverted, but when it comes to cooking, I'm a lot more self-assured. I thought it might be quite a stressful experience, but it ended up being really fun.

Interviewer: Have you ever worked in a professional kitchen?

Mike: No, but <u>I've always had the feeling that I'd open my own restaurant one day because I'm always praised for my cooking skills.</u> The closest I'd got to that was occasionally eating out in a restaurant. I've been cooking since I was a child, although it's only recently that I've become more creative with it. So I suppose that helped.

Interviewer: What was the first day in the studio like?

Mike: It was a bit nerve-racking. I hadn't read the email that had been sent to me properly and so I didn't know I'd have to cook for the judges that day. I thought we'd just be learning how the show worked and doing sound tests. <u>I had to come up with something then and there, so I baked a cake that I could remember how to make by heart.</u> It was a bit on the easy side, so I thought there was no way I'd get through to the next round. But the judges thought it was delicious and said I was in.

Interviewer: Is being on the programme as stressful as it looks on the TV?

Mike: In some ways, yes. We had the same time limits as you see on the show. We usually had an hour to cook something, but that wasn't too bad. I think it seems more stressful on the TV because of the dramatic music they use. We didn't have that, <u>but having to get used to all the equipment was tough.</u> I'm used to hanging out in my own kitchen where I know the oven temperature and where all the knives are.

Interviewer: Do people stop you in the street now?

Mike: Sometimes - and there's not much I can do about it. <u>I still find it strange that people know who I am.</u> With adults, it's different. They don't remember me from the show exactly, but they recognise my face without knowing why. People are more confused than anything. It's a bit embarrassing, but I know it's not going to last for very long.

Interviewer: What was the best thing about being on the show?

Mike: I have to say I learnt a lot about food and came out a much better cook than I went in. <u>Above all, though, I'll always cherish the friendships I made.</u> When the show's on TV, they make it look like we are all really competitive and don't get on, but that's not true at all. I'm still in touch with quite a few contestants and we've become really close thanks to our shared interest in food.

Interviewer:	So, did you win *Stars of the Kitchen* in the end?
Mike:	Well, the final episodes haven't gone to air yet so <u>I have to keep it to myself – that's part of the contract.</u> Let's just say it's going to get very exciting and there are a few shocks as well! So I'm afraid you'll just have to wait and see like everyone else. The next episode's on Wednesday night. We're going to be cooking Spanish food.
Interviewer:	I'll be watching for sure. Thanks so much for coming in, Mike.

Writing Part 2 (A review)

1 1 such 2 enough 3 meals 4 so 5 recipes 6 dish 7 food 8 too

Unit 5 Study time

Grammar
Zero, first and second conditionals

1
1 weren't
2 go
3 will/'ll need / needs
4 finish / have finished
5 choose
6 complete / have completed
7 wouldn't do
8 will/'ll try
9 don't pass
10 got /had got

2
1 correct
2 I would/'d spend more time practising
3 She will / 'll have trouble finding a job
4 he has studied / he's studied / studies too late
5 would I need to take an advanced maths course
6 correct
7 I am going to travel / I'm going to travel / I will travel / I'll travel
8 correct

Vocabulary
Phrasal verbs

1
1 look back at 2 got away with 3 puts off 4 handing back
5 live up to 6 turned out 7 pointed out 8 get over

find out, get to know, know, learn, teach and *study*; *attend, join, take part* and *assist*

2
1 ~~unite~~ join 2 ~~known~~ learned 3 ~~learn~~ study 4 ~~join~~ attend
5 ~~know~~ find out 6 ~~learned~~ taught 7 ~~know~~ get to know 8 ~~join~~ take part in

Study words

3
Across 2 career 4 degree 5 prospects 7 revision 8 tutor 9 marks
Down 1 research 2 course 3 admission 6 lessons

Suffixes

4

-tion	-ence	-ment
intention	existence	adjustment
investigation	preference	agreement
qualification		assessment
		development
		involvement

-ance	other
appearance	advice
	behaviour
	comparison
	confusion
	feeling
	response

5
1 agreement 2 comparison/confusion 3 investigation 4 preference
5 response

Listening Part 1

1 C **2** A **3** A **4** B **5** B **6** A **7** B **8** C

Track 6

Narrator:	One. You hear a father talking to his son about university.
Son:	Dad, why didn't you go to university?
Dad:	I did go for a couple of years. Didn't I ever tell you that? I started doing a degree in Accounting and I didn't do too badly in the early part of the course. <u>Then your grandfather got ill and I had to come home to run the family business.</u> I always intended to go back and finish it at some stage, but then I met your mum and you kids came along. I suppose it's a shame I didn't manage to finish my degree, but I would have ended up doing the same work anyway, so it didn't really change much.
Narrator:	Two. You hear two students talking about the university library.
Female:	When do you go to the university library? I've never seen you there.
Male:	I don't go much at all. I prefer to do all my research online. It's easier than having to ask the librarian to collect books and material for me. I have to wait, and then I take a look at them and find they don't contain the information I want at all. <u>It drives me crazy wasting so much time.</u> It's a good thing the papers I need for my research are available free online, otherwise I'd be in the library as much as you.
Narrator:	Three. You hear a student talking to a friend about his new school.
Girl:	How are you enjoying studying overseas?
Boy:	Well… it is one of the best schools in Britain, and it'll give me lots of options for my future education. Winning that scholarship to go away to school has made my parents so proud. <u>But I really struggle being so far from them and all my old friends here in New Zealand.</u>
Girl:	That's not so good. Are the lessons tough?
Boy:	Oh no, my old school must've been good, because I don't feel I'm behind in any way. Actually, I'm ahead in maths. I sometimes feel I really don't need to be there, but I wouldn't want to disappoint Mum and Dad by not giving it a chance.
Narrator	Four. You hear a student talking to a friend about a history report he has written.
Male:	Can you check this report for me?
Female:	But you know we don't cover this subject on my course.
Male:	I just need someone to read it through to make sure it sounds OK. My friend Isobel and I wrote different sections each, and <u>I'm worried it's not very clear.</u> It'd be useful to get an objective opinion to make sure it's understandable. Please! You've always helped me in the past.
Female:	OK, but I won't be checking any facts.
Male:	That's OK. Thank you so much. Feel free to write any comments you have on it. I'm sure Isobel will be just as happy as me to have another person look at it.

Reading and Use of English Part 3

1 repeatedly   **2** interested   **3** differences   **4** unmotivated / demotivated
5 comparison   **6** information   **7** creativity   **8** knowledge

Writing Part 1 (An essay)

1

<u>Giving your opinion</u>
in my opinion
I believe

<u>Introducing other people's opinions</u>
Some people think that

<u>Introducing an argument</u>
There are several reasons

<u>Expressing contrast</u>
However
on the other hand

<u>Putting your ideas in order</u>
Firstly
Furthermore

<u>Introducing your conclusion</u>
To sum up

2
1 F (You must do the essay in Part 1.)
2 F (You must cover the two points given and include your own idea as well.)
3 F
4 T
5 T
6 T
7 F (Your essay should be between 140 and 190 words.)
8 T

Unit 6 Good job!

Grammar
Countable and uncountable nouns

1
2 scenery – U   **3** idea – C   **4** favour – C   **5** luggage – U
6 music – U   **7** trip – C   **8** food – U

Articles

2
1 -   **2** -   **3** the   **4** a   **5** an   **6** -   **7** -   **8** a   **9** the   **10** the   **11** the   **12** a
13 -   **14** a   **15** a   **16** -   **17** a   **18** -   **19** the

Vocabulary
work or *job*; *possibility*, *occasion* or *opportunity*;
fun or *funny*

1
1 fascinating   **2** part-time   **3** manual   **4** outdoors
5 tiring/tough   **6** well-paid   **7** responsible   **8** hard
9 challenging   **10** demanding   **11** worthwhile   **12** permanent

2
1 I couldn't find any information online about the company.
2 correct
3 correct
4 If you get the opportunity/chance, call me tonight.
5 I spent all weekend doing geography homework.
6 Do you have any decorating equipment I can borrow?
7 I need (some) advice on how to prepare for a job interview.
8 Is there any possibility/chance you could babysit for me this evening?

Writing Part 2 (An email or letter)

1
1 T (The word limit is 190 words.)
2 T (There are no contractions, phrasal verbs or informal expressions.)
3 F (Each main point from the advertisement should be dealt with in a separate paragraph in the letter.)
4 F (The formal greeting and sign-off are *Dear Mr Davis* and *Yours sincerely*. A formal greeting should contain the surname and not the first name. If the greeting contains a person's name, the sign-off is *Yours sincerely*; if it is *Dear Sir or Madam*, the sign-off is *Yours faithfully*.)
5 T
6 F (There is no mention of the candidate's ability to communicate in English.)

2
1 H   **2** D   **3** F   **4** C   **5** B   **6** G   **7** E   **8** A

Listening Part 3

1 E   2 C   3 G   4 A   5 D

> **Track 7**
>
> **Narrator:** Speaker 1
> **Speaker 1:** After I graduated, I got a job as an accountant with a very big international firm. I'd go around to different companies checking their financial records to make sure they were paying the right amount of tax. It annoyed me when people said the job sounded boring. I remember I loved the variety and <u>the salary was more generous than I'd expected.</u> I was working at a different company every month and it was really rewarding to be able to use everything I'd learned at university. I don't work for that firm any more, but I'm still an accountant.
>
> **Narrator:** Speaker 2
> **Speaker 2:** I used to work as a lifeguard at the beach during my summers when I was at university. I had to do a short course to qualify and I also needed to know first aid. There weren't many waves and the water wasn't very deep, so not many people got into trouble. <u>As a result, it did have its dull moments.</u> For me, it was an excuse to hang out in the sunshine for the whole summer and get paid for it. The money wasn't great, but I met a lot of people, and on a few occasions, I was able to help people in the water.
>
> **Narrator:** Speaker 3
> **Speaker 3:** <u>I had trouble finding a job in the field I'd studied for. I eventually got hired as a drama teacher, but until that happened I worked in a call centre for about three years.</u> It certainly wasn't my dream job, talking to people who were complaining about their wi-fi going down, but it paid the bills at the time. It also taught me how to deal with angry customers and bring some calm to very negative situations. After a while, I just got used to it, as I knew that every call I got was an emergency situation for someone. It became easier to deal with.
>
> **Narrator:** Speaker 4
> **Speaker 4:** I worked in a nursing home for old people. It's not a job I would have done my whole life, but I'm glad I had the experience. <u>Nursing homes struggle to fill these positions, so I had no problems in finding work.</u> It certainly wasn't all fun and games, but I mainly remember the lovely old people that I cared for and how I tried to find time for them when they needed someone to talk to. I've always been a good listener. It can be difficult for people to move into a nursing home, and sometimes a bit lonely, especially in the evenings when there are fewer people for them to talk to.
>
> **Narrator:** Speaker 5
> **Speaker 5:** Cleaning people's houses was a great way to pay the bills when I was studying. It was relatively straightforward, but it was hard work. I had to clean the bathrooms and kitchens, and do all the floors. I would put on my headphones and listen to music though, and the time would fly. I could just switch off and daydream. <u>It was a good way to stay in shape, too – I remember enjoying that a lot.</u> These days I have my own house cleaned once a week because my job means I don't have time to do it myself.

Reading and Use of English Part 5

1 A   2 C   3 C   4 D   5 A   6 B

Unit 7 High adventure

Grammar
Infinitive and verb + -ing

1

1 to show	2 sitting	3 being	4 to get	5 training
6 to reduce	7 to start	8 playing	9 Joining	10 not to try

2

1 admitted	2 thought	3 failed	4 succeeded
5 avoided	6 allowed	7 expected	8 decided

Vocabulary
Verb collocations with activities

1

1 going   2 doing   3 compete in   4 playing   5 do   6 held

look, *see*, *watch*, *listen* and *hear*

2

1 to see   2 watching   3 heard   4 don't listen   5 looked   6 watching

3

1 ~~saw~~ looked	2 correct	3 correct	4 ~~listen to~~ hear
5 ~~watched~~ saw	6 ~~listened to~~ heard	7 correct	8 ~~watched~~ saw

Reading and Use of English Part 4

1 suggested taking | an
2 win | despite having
3 any people / anybody / anyone | swam there
4 find it | annoying
5 gets by | on
6 had his | blood pressure checked

Listening Part 4

1 B   2 A   3 B   4 C   5 A   6 B   7 A

> **Track 8**
>
> **Narrator:** You will hear an interview with a motorcycle racer called Darren Beanhill. For questions 1 to 7, choose the best answer (A, B or C).
> **Interviewer:** Today I'm interviewing the young motorcycle racer Darren Beanhill. Welcome Darren. You've been racing for a few years now. Can you remember your first ever race?
> **Darren:** I grew up on a farm in Australia, so I was riding motorcycles from the age of seven. When I was 12, there was a race put on in my town for under-16s. I thought, well, I'm under 16 so I should qualify. <u>All the boys there were bigger and had really expensive, new bikes. I just turned up with one we had used on the farm for years and everyone thought it was hilarious.</u> They didn't tease me for long, though. I ended up winning the race, despite my age.
> **Interviewer:** This is your third year on the international circuit. How is it different from your first two years?
> **Darren:** I think people know now that I stay in the middle of the pack for most of the race and then start overtaking in the last ten minutes. The first year I was the new kid in town and that was a big advantage. I've been threatening to get into the top five for the past couple of years, <u>so now other riders see I'm real competition for them.</u> I don't worry about what the other riders think of me – I'm concentrating too hard on getting to the finish line as fast as I can.
> **Interviewer:** You had some trouble with your tyres last year. How is it going this season?

Darren:	Last year they were new tyres for me, and I had some problems with the grip, especially in the rain. <u>I'm slowly getting used to them, and that's given me added confidence on the bends.</u> It's amazing how much a tyre can affect your whole performance, but I suppose they're my only point of contact with the track – it all starts from there, doesn't it?
Interviewer:	You spend much of the year at races around the world. How do you cope with the lifestyle?
Darren:	Apart from the racing, I live a pretty normal life. My wife and my son, Ricky, travel with me, and we tend to avoid hotel rooms and find somewhere to stay that is more like home. Sure, we're not in one place for very long, <u>but there's something very calming about having both of them with me.</u> I don't know what's going to happen when Ricky has to start going to school, but that's not for a year or two yet.
Interviewer:	How would you describe a typical motorbike racer?
Darren:	Well, we all seem to have a way of blocking fear. I'm aware of the dangers, but <u>all the riders at this professional level love speed and none of us is concerned about coming off,</u> or even crashing into fellow riders, for that matter. If I suddenly became anxious about going out there, I'd have to quit racing. I've seen it happen to some of my peers. It's meant the end of their careers.
Interviewer:	Do you have an age you'd like to retire at?
Darren:	I'm 24. Nowadays people are racing until they're nearly 40. Who knows where I'll be and what I'll be doing at that age. Right now, I love it, and I'm just living from season to season. I certainly don't want to think about quitting before I've won a championship. But there's not just yourself to consider when you're married. <u>My wife and I will determine that together, when the time comes.</u>
Interviewer:	The forecast says it's going to be 38 °C for the race on Sunday. Will that affect your performance?
Darren:	It'll probably help me, in fact. All the races in this championship are in hot places – we follow the sun around the world all year and our bikes are designed to cope. Add in the fact that I'm Australian and grew up in the heat, so I'm used to racing in high temperatures. <u>It's a positive factor for me, unlike the riders who come from cooler climates</u> – I don't have to adapt. In fact, it's when it's cold and raining that my performance is weakest.
Interviewer:	Thank you for coming in today.
Darren:	Thank you.

Writing Part 2 (An article)

1 In addition **2** As a result **3** As well as
4 By doing this **5** Moreover **6** also

Unit 8 Dream of the stars

Grammar

at, in and on in phrases expressing location

1
1 on, at **2** at, in **3** in **4** on **5** at **6** on **7** at **8** in

Reported speech

2
2 It's the funniest film I've ever seen.
3 I've never heard of it.
4 I'll/I'd definitely watch it again.
5 I can't see it because I don't live near a cinema. / I couldn't see it because I don't live near a cinema.
6 I didn't really enjoy it because it was too long.

Reporting verbs

3
2 promise **3** admit **4** apologise **5** recommend **6** agree **7** warn

4
2 Oliver admitted that it was him who had broken the mirror.
3 My husband agreed that we could go out that night.
4 Julia apologised for not seeing my performance the day before / yesterday.
5 William promised that he would be on time the next day / tomorrow.
6 Angelo recommended that I/we should stream the TV series.
7 Lisa warned us not to buy concert tickets from strangers.

Vocabulary

Describing entertainment

1
Across	**4** play	**5** gripping	**8** stage	**12** audience
	14 famous	**16** edge of your seat	**17** scene	**18** musical
Down	**1** rerun	**2** twist	**3** part	**6** predictable
	7 performance	**9** act	**10** spectators	**11** binge watch
	12 audition	**13** hilarious	**15** hooked	

Listening Part 2

1 father	**2** communication	**3** level	**4** style	**5** contacts
6 reputation	**7** tips	**8** novels	**9** flexible	**10** professional

---

Track 9

Narrator: You will hear a woman called Margie Levine talking about her job as a Hollywood agent. For questions 1 to 10, complete the sentences with a word or short phrase.

Speaker: I've been an agent for actors in Hollywood for nearly 30 years and I've worked with the best in the world. I had an interest in acting from a young age. Show business was in the family – my aunt was a backing dancer in several classical musicals in the 50s. I even tried to pursue a career in musical theatre myself – against the advice of my <u>father</u> – but that came to an end pretty quickly as I wasn't that good at singing or dancing.

But I never lost my desire to work in a creative industry, I just needed to find something that matched my skills. Effective <u>communication</u> has always been one of my strengths and a friend who was working as a talent agent said this quality would make me perfect for that role. You're dealing with dozens of people on a day-to-day basis, so you have to be able to express yourself clearly. I had to learn to be a little more diplomatic, especially when turning actors down, but this came with time.

So I started at the bottom, as a receptionist for a big firm in Los Angeles. Then I became an assistant, then an agent, then a head of department. By holding various positions at each <u>level</u> of the firm, I got to understand completely how it operated. It was a long, slow learning process, but I got the best possible training in the industry.

I never had the intention of starting my own agency, but I kept meeting actors that I liked who were really talented and that I wanted to represent. However, they didn't fit in with the company's <u>style</u>. So I took a chance and started out on my own. It was a bit of a culture shock at first, working alone and not having anyone else to rely on. However, since I had so much experience and so many <u>contacts</u> in the industry, it didn't take me long to become established and get offered lots of assignments.

Once I was working with actors whose abilities I was sure of, I was able to get them plenty of work. This helped me develop my <u>reputation</u> as a talent agent and gain the trust of casting directors, who knew I would only send actors of a high standard.

Young actors are always asking me for <u>tips</u> on how to succeed in Hollywood. I usually give them three. The main thing is that you need to keep developing your skills. Just because you've finished drama school, it doesn't mean your training is over. You never know what you're going to be cast in as an actor and you have to be ready for anything. If you're well-prepared, you'll be less nervous.

Take regular acting classes, learn languages, learn to ride a horse, learn to fight, familiarise yourself with the most recent <u>novels</u>.

Secondly, you have to bear in mind that the best actor doesn't always get the job, so selling yourself well is the first step. By selling yourself, I mean not just showing that you're talented when you audition, but that you're a team player and can get on well with people. Most importantly, however, you have to show that you are <u>flexible</u> when the need arises. The most successful Hollywood actors are the least demanding. That's no coincidence. Casting directors give jobs to people who are going to make their lives easier and not cause problems.

The third suggestion is to make the most of your promotional materials. Don't get your photographs taken by a friend – go to a <u>professional</u>. Amateur-looking photos create a terrible first impression. Keep your biography up to date. After you have an audition, the people in casting will look at your social media. Does it represent the sort of person a film or TV production would want to hire?

So if your agent gives you advice, take it. It's in their interest to find you work, so trust what they say. They know the business.

Reading and Use of English Part 7

1 C 2 B 3 B 4 C 5 D 6 A 7 D 8 C 9 B 10 A

Reading and Use of English Part 1

1 B 2 D 3 B 4 A 5 C 6 A 7 C 8 D

Writing Part 1 (An essay)

1 One of the main reasons is 2 Because of this 3 for this reason
4 Because / Since 5 That is why 6 because / since

Unit 9 The power of the mind

Grammar
Modal verbs to express certainty and possibility

1
2 She might/could/may be out with her friends.
3 He might not/may not speak English.
4 That must be fun.
5 It can't be him driving that car.
6 Her parents must have been very proud of her.
7 They can't have bought another one.
8 My mother might have/may have/could have cooked it for me when I was young.
9 She can't have been able to write.
10 They might/may/could have thought I couldn't afford it.

2
1 can't 2 might/could 3 can't 4 could 5 must 6 may/might

Vocabulary
achieve, carry out and *devote*; *stay, spend* and *pass*; *make, cause* and *have*

1
1 spending 2 stay 3 spend 4 stay 5 passed 6 spend
2
1 f 2 a 3 d 4 e 5 c 6 b
3

achieve	carry out	devote
an ambition an objective success	an improvement an instruction an objective an order research a test a threat	energy to one's life to time to

Reading and Use of English Part 4

1 can't | be switched
2 I came | across
3 is much | tastier than
4 warned me | not to go
5 will go on | until
6 shouldn't | have borrowed

Listening Part 1

1 B 2 C 3 A 4 C 5 B 6 A 7 B 8 C

Track 10

Narrator: One. You hear a man talking about drinking coffee.

Man: One of the great pleasures in my life is my first coffee of the day. I'm quite fussy about it. Of course, it can't be instant coffee – in fact, I'm not very keen on any coffee I make myself. I've experimented with most home gadgets and machines, and <u>found that nothing comes close to what a café coffee machine can produce.</u> Luckily, there's a café in my street that I can go to every morning. If I want to fit in a coffee before work, it has the added benefit of making me get up and get dressed on time.

Narrator: Two. You hear a father talking to his son.

Father: Wake up, Jack! It's ten o'clock already and it's a beautiful day outside.

Son: Aaagh … Dad, it's Sunday – let me sleep in. It's the only day I can do it.

Father: <u>I think you're wasting the day.</u> I know you have to study a lot, but why waste the free time you do have lying in bed?

Son: This is the only day I've got that's truly mine. I love sleeping in…

Father: I've been up since six. I've already taken the dog for a walk and done a load of washing. You've lost half the day already.

Son: Come on, Dad! I'm sure you loved sleeping in when you were my age.

Narrator: Three. You hear a woman talking about doing yoga.

Woman: When I tell people how much I love yoga, <u>I always get the feeling they think it's some kind of passive relaxation therapy.</u> The reality is that the hour I spend twice a week in my yoga class really pushes my body to the limit – <u>it calls for a lot of energy and movement.</u> Everyone knows that all that stretching releases chemicals in the body called endorphins that have a real calming effect. But the body reacts in this way for a reason: it needs to balance out the stress that it undergoes when you hold a yoga position for a long time.

Narrator:	Four. You hear a man and a woman meeting after a long time.
Woman:	Is that you, James?
Man:	Christine? Wow, how long has it been? It must be ten years!
Woman:	Yes! Is this your usual supermarket? How strange I've never run into you in here before.
Man:	I only moved back to the area last month. I realised I could do my job anywhere and I was getting sick of city life. I've been wondering who still lives here.
Woman:	I'm still living with my parents. I travel a lot for work, so it hasn't been worth getting my own place. <u>There aren't many from our class still in the village, though.</u>
Man:	That's a shame. It would have been nice to catch up with old friends.
Narrator:	Five. You hear a man talking about a favourite pair of trainers.
Man:	I think I've had these trainers for about ten years, and I'd love to wear them every day. They've faded quite a bit, so you can tell they aren't new, but they haven't got any holes or tears in them. The fact is, though, that they don't exactly look like they've just come out the box, I don't mind. The most important thing is they're comfortable. I can put them on and know I'm not going to have any problems with them. <u>Unfortunately, they aren't smart enough for work.</u> I mean… I don't care how I look, but the boss does.
Narrator:	Six. You hear a man and a woman talking about a film they've just seen.
Man:	I'm not sure if it was worth spending three hours of my time watching that film.
Woman:	I loved the storyline. I think it was really clever how they revealed who the murderer was.
Man:	I guessed who it was quite early, actually. The guy who played the main role did really well – he has such an expressive face.
Woman:	He did give a very impressive performance. I loved the music, too.
Man:	I'm not sure about having a classical soundtrack in a film like this, but I can see why you liked it. For me, it just didn't work in this film.
Narrator:	Seven. You hear a student who's worried about planning her study time.
Woman:	I'm just under so much stress at the moment. I have university exams coming up and I really don't know how I'm going to study properly for everything. I still have classes to go to and I'm working every evening as a waitress. I need to ask my boss if I can take some time off to study, or at least reduce my hours, but I'm worried I might lose my job. <u>Strange that I'm more anxious about my part-time job than university</u> – my exams really need to come first. I should consider a less demanding job.
Narrator:	Eight. You hear a woman giving a talk about meditation.
Woman:	I was suffering terrible mood swings and was always exhausted, so a friend suggested I try meditation. Even though I was doubtful it would help, I was willing to give it a go. It wasn't easy getting in a comfortable position or clearing my brain of my thoughts. Some days I suspected I was wasting my time, but eventually I was able to do it. It might not be the solution for everyone, but it really calmed me down. Not just that, but <u>my memory improved</u> – <u>I started planning my life more effectively and generally felt more positive.</u> Now I wish I'd taken that up years ago.

Writing Part 2 (A report)

1
Sentences 2, 3, 5 and 6 should be ticked

2
1 to find   2 opening   3 repairing   4 to close   5 to attract   6 building

Unit 10 Spend, spend, spend

Grammar
as and *like*

1
1 as   2 correct   3 correct   4 like   5 correct   6 correct   7 as   8 like

Modal verbs to express ability

2
1 can't / 'm not able to / won't be able to
2 couldn't / wasn't able to
3 can
4 haven't been able to
5 could already / was already able to
6 Will I be able to
7 could have
8 am always able to / have always been able to / can always

Vocabulary
arrive, get and *reach*

1
1 arrived   2 reached   3 arriving   4 get   5 arrives   6 arrive / get

2
1 bargain	2 brand	3 sale	4 competitive	5 consumer
6 available	7 stock	8 purchase	9 counter	10 debit card

Phrasal verbs

3
1 for	2 in	3 over	4 into	5 up	6 out
7 up	8 up	9 down	10 around	11 out	12 up

Reading and Use of English Part 2

1 into/in   2 so   3 what   4 even   5 having   6 front   7 there   8 been

Listening Part 4

1 A   2 C   3 A   4 A   5 B   6 B   7 C

Track 11	
Narrator:	You will hear a radio interview with a personal shopper called Amanda Houseman. For questions 1 to 7, choose the best answer (A, B or C).
Interviewer:	Today, I have with me Amanda Houseman, who will be talking to me about her job as a personal shopper. First of all, Amanda, what does a personal shopper do?
Amanda:	I help busy people who need to buy clothes but never get the chance. Finding time to go shopping is tough for many professional people today, <u>so my principal role is solving that problem.</u> I put together a selection of clothing, usually a mix of luxury, high-prized designer items and everyday brands, which I take to clients to try on. Then they choose what they'd like to buy and I take the other clothes back to the shop.
Interviewer:	What kind of experience do you need for the job?
Amanda:	Well, time spent employed in the fashion industry is a good start. <u>I began by working in a department store.</u> That doesn't sound like much, but apart from serving customers I built up a lot of skills, including getting to know the work of different designers and learning about sizes and fabrics. Some people have a degree in fashion, and I imagine that would be useful, too.

Interviewer: How did you make the change to being a personal shopper?

Amanda: A customer at the place I was working wanted some advice on what she should take on a business trip. What I chose for her must have been right because not only did she buy everything I suggested, she also offered to pay me to choose clothes for her regularly. I started shopping for her in my spare time, and people began asking her where she got her clothes. That's how it started. She passed my name on to anyone who was interested and I slowly built up a business.

Interviewer: How do you know what clothes to take to clients?

Amanda: Often I'll just get a picture in my head of what they need, or I may spot something in a shop and think that's perfect for a particular person. But in the beginning, much of it is getting to know the individual. I always sit down with them and ask questions about their work and lifestyle. I like to visit clients at home as I can usually learn more about their tastes from the way their house is decorated than from what they're wearing. Just doing that, you get to know a lot about them.

Interviewer: What problems come with the job?

Amanda: It sometimes worries me having to handle clothes that are worth so much. The clothes are my responsibility once they leave the store, so there's quite a bit of trust involved with clients. I once had a client who didn't pay me for the clothes that she'd kept, so that has made me rather cautious. Since then I've only worked for people who have been recommended to me by other clients.

Interviewer: Do you ever take the clients shopping with you?

Amanda: They sometimes ask, but I try to avoid it – above all because when I'm out shopping it's usually for more than one person, so it wouldn't be an efficient way for me to work. Also, if you're in a shop with a client, you lose control of the situation and they can start trying on things that aren't right for them. I don't discourage them from making their own selections, it's their money after all, but it does mean that I have to find something there and then which suits them better.

Interviewer: What advice would you give someone who wants to be a personal shopper?

Amanda: You need to have confidence in your ability to choose the right clothes and be able to guide people without pushing them too hard. On the other hand, you can't forget you have to be flexible, too. If a client doesn't like what you've brought them, it can be quite tough turning round and going out shopping for them again. You need to be ready to admit you might have got the selection wrong. In the end, the client has to want to wear the clothes you've chosen.

Writing Part 2 (A review)

1
2 It was the cover of the book that
3 What I found out when I started reading it was that
4 It was the description of life in New Orleans that
5 What I really liked about this book was that it
6 What I want to read next is

2
1 What I really need at the moment is a new tablet.
2 It was Michael who stole the book from the shop.
3 What happens is the main character loses his job.
4 It was last year that she took out a bank loan.
5 It was the black shoes which I liked the most.
6 What I don't know is what time the department store opens.

Unit 11 Medical matters

Grammar
Relative pronouns and relative clauses

1a
1 which 2 whose 3 who 4 which 5 where
6 which 7 which 8 whose 9 who 10 which

1b
5 I like going to places like the beach in winter, where I know there won't be many people.
7 The city's football team, which is at the top of the league, has more fans than any other.

1c
The relative pronouns can be replaced by *that* in 1, 3, 4, 6, 9 and 10.

1d
The relative pronouns can be omitted in 4 and 10.

2
1 f   2 c   3 d   4 a   5 e   6 b

Vocabulary
Words relating to health

1
Across	1 itchy	4 bumped	7 sneezing	8 broke
	9 reaction	10 feet	12 coughing	
Down	1 injured	2 stung	3 weather	5 poisoning
	6 bug	8 bled	11 hurt	

Word formation

2
1 ability   2 awareness   3 certainty   4 experience   5 formality
6 happiness   7 helpfulness   8 honesty   9 patience   10 possibility
11 predictability   12 reliability   13 satisfaction

3
dis-	im-	in-	un-
dishonest dissatisfied	impatient impossible	inexperienced informal	unable unaware uncertain unhappy unhelpful unpredictable unreliable unsatisfied

Listening Part 3

1 F   2 C   3 H   4 D   5 B

Track 12

Narrator: Speaker 1

Speaker 1: At around the age of ten I wanted to be an Olympic swimmer. Hours spent in the pool had me getting some really good times for my age and I was competing at regional level. The dream ended, however, after a stay in hospital for a particularly nasty ear infection. It left me almost unable to hear in one ear. The doctor told me it was simply too risky getting back in the pool again, so I had to give up swimming. Still determined, I took up cricket instead, and with the same crazy enthusiasm I'd had for the pool. I got better and better, and now I play for my county.

Narrator: Speaker 2

Speaker 2: You know lice, the little insects that live in your hair? I had them when I was seven. When I turned up at school with an extremely short haircut and parents were told that they needed to check their kids' heads, fingers were soon pointed at me. School was a nightmare after that. <u>Nobody would play with me and some kids were even afraid of me. I was miserable.</u> I really think the teacher should have stepped in at this point and explained to the class that I didn't have lice any more. It wasn't until I went to secondary school that it was all forgotten.

Narrator: Speaker 3

Speaker 3: Children can get vaccinated for it now, but when I was young, chickenpox was a disease everyone got at some point in their childhood. I woke up one morning covered from head to toe in itchy red spots. It made them worse if I scratched them, but I just couldn't resist it, so my mum had to wrap my hands in bandages to stop me. <u>The one thing that worked was lying in a cool bath.</u> Nothing else seemed to help. I was ill for about two weeks – it was terrible. I think it's great that kids don't suffer as much from this illness these days.

Narrator: Speaker 4

Speaker 4: My parents always made me put on sunscreen at the beach, as I had really fair skin. But one day I went with a friend and his family and <u>though Mom had sent me off with a bottle of sunscreen, I forgot to put it on.</u> I had to spend the next three days lying on my stomach as my back and shoulders were really badly sunburnt – I got incredibly painful blisters. I certainly learnt my lesson. Now, when it's hot, I don't leave the house without putting sunscreen on. I never want to go through that again!

Narrator: Speaker 5

Speaker 5: One morning, I woke up completely unable to speak. I had laryngitis, a throat infection. It didn't hurt and I felt OK, so I went to school anyway. My parents didn't think to give me a note for the teacher. Probably because I looked fine, she wasn't convinced that I had really lost my voice, and thought I was just playing games with her. As the morning went on and I still didn't speak, she lost her patience with me and sent me to the headteacher. <u>It wasn't until the headteacher had phoned my parents that I was allowed back into class.</u>

Reading and Use of English Part 6

1 G   2 E   3 A   4 C   5 F   6 D

Writing Part 1 (An essay)

1 due to
2 despite
3 Although / Even though
4 however

5 whereas / while
6 While / Whereas
7 Even though / Although
8 but

1
1 in spite of knowing (that)
2 While it's important to

3 even though they know (that)
4 the fact that temperatures drop

Unit 12 Animal kingdom

Grammar
Third and mixed conditionals

1
1 hadn't gone, wouldn't have found
2 wouldn't have seen, hadn't taken
3 wouldn't have discovered, hadn't offered
4 wouldn't be, hadn't quit

wish, *if only* and *hope*

2
| 1 If only | 2 hope | 3 wish | 4 hope | 5 hope |
| 6 wish | 7 If only | 8 hope | 9 wish | 10 wish |

3
1 correct
2 hadn't had the binoculars with her
3 I wish I/we had seen more elephants
4 correct
5 so I hope
6 correct
7 it hadn't rained
8 we could stay

Vocabulary
avoid, *prevent* and *protect*; *check*, *control*, *keep an eye on* and *supervise*

1
| 1 protect | 2 supervised | 3 prevent | 4 avoid |
| 5 control | 6 check | 7 keep an eye on | |

Reading and Use of English Part 7

1 C   2 D   3 B   4 A   5 C   6 A   7 C   8 A   9 D   10 B

Reading and Use of English Part 1

1 A   2 C   3 A   4 D   5 B   6 D   7 B   8 C

Listening Part 1

1 C   2 A   3 A   4 A   5 B   6 B   7 A   8 C

Track 13	
Narrator:	One. You hear a man speaking to his friend about a neighbour's pet bird.
Woman:	What's that whistling sound?
Man:	It's the bird that lives upstairs. The lady that owns it puts the cage out on her balcony if it's a nice day. That's why you can hear it.
Woman:	Why would anyone want to have a bird? It seems cruel to me, never letting it out of a cage.
Man:	Does it sound unhappy to you? It sings like that all day. <u>My neighbour lives by herself and she says it keeps her company.</u> She told me she sometimes lets it out of the cage and it flies round the house. Apparently, it goes back to its cage on its own when it's had enough.
Woman:	Really?

Narrator:	Two. You hear a mother talking to her son about an incident at the beach.
Mother:	Why are you back from the beach so early? Are you OK?
Son:	Well … I was sitting on my surfboard in the water when a shark started circling me. I was too afraid to use my arms to get back to shore, so I had to wait for the next wave and surfed in on my stomach.
Mother:	That's unbelievable! You weren't in the water on your own, were you?
Son:	Of course not. I shouted to my friends and they got out quickly as well.
Mother:	I thought they fly a helicopter over that beach checking for sharks.
Son:	Only at the weekend.
Mother:	Well, you're not to go there unless it's the weekend, then.
Narrator:	Three. You hear a man talking to his friend about a dog walking service.
Man:	I've recently started using a dog walking service.
Woman:	Oh really, what's it like?
Man:	Well, I was a little hesitant at first because it's surprisingly pricey, but then I made a few savings elsewhere and that made it more manageable. But it gives me peace of mind to know that someone's looking after my dog while I'm busy at work, so it's worth every penny. I do have to go a little out of my way to drop the dog off every morning before heading to the office, but it's lovely when I come back and see her so happy in the evening.
Narrator:	Four. You hear two friends talking about their exam results.
Boy:	So, how did you get on?
Girl:	Pretty good overall, I think. I wasn't expecting to do as well as I did in maths. I didn't feel at all confident coming out of the exam.
Boy:	That was one of my worst results, to be honest – although it's hardly surprising given how little time I had to prepare for it.
Girl:	But you still passed! So you must feel pretty good about that.
Boy:	You're right, I suppose. I'm just glad it's all over and I won't have to sit an exam again for a while.
Girl:	I couldn't agree with you more on that. Now we can enjoy the rest of the summer.
Narrator:	Five. You overhear a father and daughter talking on the train.
Father:	I'm glad we decided to go by train today. I'd forgotten how stunning the countryside was around here. You don't see this from the motorway.
Daughter:	Yes, it's nice, I suppose, but what are we going to do when we get to the station?
Father:	We'll take the underground. It's not far to Covent Garden.
Daughter:	Well, at least you don't have to pay for parking.
Father:	True, although I knew the train tickets wouldn't be cheap. But this way, I don't have the stress of getting stuck in traffic and arriving late. We couldn't have driven into the centre anyway – it's just not worth taking the car to London these days.
Narrator:	Six. You hear a woman talking on a radio programme about personal challenges.
Woman:	I'd been practising for months, but I was still concerned I might not be successful. My instructor told me not to worry – all I had to do was control my nerves on the day and I'd be fine. I just kept thinking of all the things that could go wrong, though. But as soon as I went outside and got behind the wheel, I felt a boost of confidence, and everything I had been practising just came naturally. The next 40 minutes flew by and when the examiner told me I'd passed, I felt so relieved – I wouldn't have been able to start my new job without my licence.

Narrator:	Seven. You hear a blind man talking about his guide dog, Lola.
Man:	I've had this guide dog, Lola, for eight years, so she's getting near retirement age. She's my fourth guide dog and I think she's the best one I've had. She never gets distracted when we're out in the street. She even ignores children trying to feed her. I have the option of keeping her here with me after I get a new dog, and in the past I've done that and had two dogs at the same time, one working and one in retirement. But I don't think I'll be able to manage this time. I'm too old now to look after two dogs.
Narrator:	Eight. You hear a man talking to an employee of a cruise company.
Man:	I'd like to change one of the names of the travellers in my booking. My wife has to work and can't come with me, so I'm taking my son instead.
Woman:	Certainly. Can you tell me the name of the passenger who's currently booked?
Man:	Yes, it's Jane Sinclair. And my son's name is Hamish Sinclair.
Woman:	OK, that shouldn't be a problem. There'll be a fee of £200 to alter the booking.
Man:	Did you say £200? You're just typing my son's name into a computer! Can't I change it myself online?
Woman:	I'm afraid that's not possible, sir.
Man:	In that case, forget it. That's simply ridiculous!

Writing Part 2 (An email)

2
1 ✓ She thinks it's a brilliant idea.
2 ✓ She suggests a dog.
3 ✓ good exercise and teaches responsibility
4 ✓ She thinks it's a good idea but warns him that pets are a big commitment.

3
Suggested places for paragraphs to begin:
[Getting a dog …, [I don't think you should get a pet…, [So, overall, I think … , [Let me know…

4
The email is too long: it is over 190 words. It should be between 140 and 190 words. There is a greeting ('Hi Jonathan') and a sign-off ('Write soon').

5
1 B   **2** D   **3** G   **4** H   **5** A   **6** E   **7** C   **8** F

Unit 13 House space

Grammar
Causative *have* and *get*

1a
2 She needs to have/get the floor carpeted.
3 She'd like to have/get the windows cleaned.
4 She has to have/get the light fixed.
5 She wants to have/get some pictures hung.
6 She is going to have/get some furniture delivered.

1b
2 She has (already) had/got the floor carpeted.
3 She has (already) had/got the windows cleaned.
4 She has (already) had/got the light fixed.
5 She hasn't had/got any pictures hung (yet).
6 She has (already) had/got some furniture delivered.

Expressing obligation and permission

2

1 I don't let my children	**5** shouldn't
2 don't have to	**6** weren't allowed to
3 needn't have planted	**7** can't
4 are not supposed to	**8** are allowed to

Vocabulary
Describing where you live

1

1 residential	**2** central	**3** neighbours	**4** outside	**5** peaceful
6 en-suite	**7** open-plan	**8** balcony	**9** links	**10** amenities

space, place, room, area, location and *square*

2

1 area	**2** room	**3** space	**4** place
5 location	**6** square	**7** place	**8** space

Listening Part 2

1 mother	**2** training	**3** certificate	**4** honesty	**5** financial situation
6 (current) owners	**7** patience	**8** plumbing	**9** 2.5 million	**10** lawyers

Track 14

Narrator: You will hear a woman called Julie Marshall talking about her work as an estate agent selling houses and other properties. For questions 1 to 10, complete the sentences with a word or short phrase.

Speaker: Hello, my name is Julie Marshall and I'm here today to talk about my job as an estate agent. I'd often thought about doing the same kind of work as my father – he was an estate agent for 30 years – but it was when we were selling the house that belonged to my grandmother that my <u>mother</u> convinced me I'd be really good at it. Some people are in it for the money, of course, and that can be a great part of the job, but I was initially interested in my company because they provided <u>training</u>, which meant I wouldn't have the expense of going to university. After just 12 months, I finished my course and passed all my exams. The company was really pleased with my performance and my boss hung my <u>certificate</u> on the wall in the office. This gave me the incentive to try for a bonus by selling properties for higher than the expected price.

The thing I love most about working with my colleagues in the agency is that we have such good communication. They're always teaching me new sales techniques and better ways to work with clients. And <u>honesty</u> with clients will always work in your favour. People will come back to you the next time they want to buy or sell a house because they have that connection. Sometimes I need information from clients that can be quite private, but thankfully personal questions about their profession are largely irrelevant nowadays. One thing I can't avoid, though, is enquiring about their <u>finances</u> if I want to show them houses they can afford.

When I'm showing the houses, I'm always amazed by what the buyers want to know. Apart from the value of the home, you'd think they'd want to know about the condition of the house, but usually they want to know about the <u>current owners</u>. Some people spend ages deciding which house they want to buy and often ask to go back for multiple viewings. I understand that. After all, buying a house is the biggest expense most people have in their lives and they want to make the right decision. So <u>patience</u> is something I have to have a lot of, even if I don't always have the enthusiasm. If you pressure people to make a decision too early, they might decide to go to another agency instead.

Sometimes people expect you to know everything about a building. I once had a couple who were very interested in an apartment I was showing them in the city centre. They had the electrics checked, and those did need some work before the purchase, but two months after they'd moved in they had problems with the <u>plumbing</u> and expected me to take care of it. It took a lot of explaining before they understood it wasn't actually my responsibility. The most expensive place I've sold was a huge beachside residence, but that needed a lot of work doing to it, so it took a long time to sell. Eventually the right buyer came along and we did the deal. I was thrilled because the agency's record for a sale was 2 million and I managed to close for <u>2.5 million</u>. It was still a bargain for the buyers because the property was originally listed for 3 million before I talked the owners into dropping the price.

I think that the most difficult part of being an estate agent isn't dealing with the homeowners, or even with the sometimes very demanding buyers, but the people that work for them. The banks can be very hard to deal with, but the toughest are the <u>lawyers</u> who inspect the contracts. They always want to change something, which means we need to get legal advice, too. But there isn't anything I can't manage – I love matching people with their perfect home and can't see myself ever doing a different job.

Writing Part 2 (An article)

1

1 No, the title is not catchy or interesting as it repeats the words in the question.
2 ✓ (It includes a question in the first paragraph.)
3 ✓
4 ✓
5 ✓ It gives an opinion in the third paragraph, but there could be a better balance between comment and description.
6 ✓

2

1 E **2** C **3** B **4** A **5** D

Reading and Use of English Part 5

1 C **2** B **3** D **4** A **5** C **6** A

Unit 14 Fiesta!

Grammar
The passive

1

1 has been held	**9** were worn
2 is surrounded	**10** were hidden
3 was set up	**11** are still worn
4 was built	**12** is attended
5 be cultivated	**13** are sold
6 were grown	**14** are also crushed
7 were employed	**15** has now been converted / is now converted
8 is still held	

The passive with reporting verbs

2

2 It is believed that the escaped prisoner is still in the area. / The escaped prisoner is believed to still be in the area.
3 It is expected that unemployment will fall next year. / Unemployment is expected to fall next year.
4 It is thought that storms will probably hit the coast on Sunday.
5 Maria Callas is considered to be the most popular opera singer ever.
6 It has been confirmed that a man (who has been) missing for 10 years has been found on a desert island. / A man missing for 10 years is confirmed to have been found on a desert island.

Vocabulary
Describing festivals and celebrations

1
1 dress up, wear **2** celebrate, commemorate **3** march, gather round
4 hold, let off **5** perform, play

Suffixes

2
1 motorist, tourist, economist, <u>refugee</u>
2 <u>researcher</u>, collector, survivor, investigator
3 consultant, <u>conductor</u>, assistant, contestant
4 salesman/woman, sportsman/woman, businessman/woman, <u>manager</u>
5 specialist, novelist, <u>comedian</u>, pharmacist
6 waiter, <u>sailor</u>, farmer, miner

Listening Part 4

1 B **2** C **3** B **4** B **5** C **6** A **7** B

Track 15

Narrator: You will hear an interview with Margaret Blake, a teacher who organises a poetry festival for young people. For questions 1 to 7, choose the best answer (A, B or C).

Interviewer: Welcome, Margaret. This year's Youth Poetry Festival starts next week. Didn't it all begin with a group of your students?

Margaret: Yes, it did. About ten years ago, I came across some poetry online and recognised the names of a few of my secondary school students, who seemed to have some sort of poetry club. They weren't doing it as classwork, so I had no idea that it was going on. <u>Apart from them putting the poems online, what really amazed me was they were also reading poems to each other at meetings they organised.</u> There was really no other means for them to do this.

Interviewer: Is this what made you come up with the idea for a poetry festival?

Margaret: That's right, it got me thinking. I had a group of students who were writing poetry because they wanted to! <u>I wondered if there was a greater movement of teens writing poetry, hungry for an audience.</u> Perhaps we could set up some sort of writers' festival? I went online to where the young people's poetry was being uploaded and asked anyone who'd like to be involved in a festival to contact me.

Interviewer: Did you get much response?

Margaret: I was completely overwhelmed with emails. I found out that there was a huge community of young poets out there. I received enquiries from all over the country <u>but wasn't expecting so much interest from people in the local area.</u> People were just so thankful for the opportunity. I even had emails from a number of poets offering to promote the festival for me, although this wasn't necessary as a colleague had already promised to set up a website.

Interviewer: So how did the first year of the festival go?

Margaret: In our first year, we had fifty young poets performing and got a lot of interest from the media. Most of the poets were from the UK, but a few had come from all around the world. <u>That's when I knew that we were really onto something big, knowing that so many young poets were willing to come all that way to read their poems in a café.</u> It also turned out to be a wonderful opportunity for them to meet and exchange ideas, so not only was it well received by the audiences, but the poets really got something out of it, too.

Interviewer: So, do you think the festival will change in the future?

Margaret: We're the biggest youth poetry festival in the country, and the event continues to grow. We've increased the number of venues to include five more coffee shops. We could include larger venues as well, but then we'd risk losing the personal atmosphere that you get in a small setting. There's been some call to incorporate short stories and songwriting, but I think we'll leave that to other festivals. <u>What would be really useful, though, is to extend the duration of the festival – we're starting to struggle to fit everyone into the schedule.</u>

Interviewer: If listeners can't get to the festival, is there anywhere they can read the poems?

Margaret: Each year we publish a book with all the poems from that year's festival, along with a short biography of each young poet. <u>The tenth edition came out yesterday, and you can order it online.</u> Be quick, though, as copies usually run out quite quickly. But I really think that people should come along to the performances and hear them in person.

Interviewer: And what about your original poets from ten years ago?

Margaret: Some of them are involved in the organisation of this year's festival. <u>You have to be between 15 and 25 years old to enter, so they can't take part as they're beyond the age limit.</u> They all tell me they still write poetry. I'm not sure whether they still meet to read it – I should ask. But if anyone's interested, the opening night is this Saturday. Just go to our website to check the venues. It's youngpoetsfestival.com.

Interviewer: It all sounds very exciting. Thank you for coming in, Margaret.

Reading and Use of English Part 6

1 B **2** E **3** G **4** D **5** A **6** C

Reading and Use of English Part 3

1 competition **2** innovative **3** fashionable **4** responsibility
5 artistic **6** annually **7** achievements **8** exchange

Writing Part 1 (An essay)

1
1 D **2** B **3** A **4** C

Acknowledgements

The authors and publishers acknowledge the following sources of copyright material and are grateful for the permissions granted. While every effort has been made, it has not always been possible to identify the sources of all the material used, or to trace all copyright holders. If any omissions are brought to our notice, we will be happy to include the appropriate acknowledgements on reprinting and in the next update to the digital edition, as applicable.

Key: U = Unit

Photography

The following images have been sourced from Getty Images.

U1: franckreporter/E+; FG Trade/E+; FatCamera/E+; Thomas Barwick/Stone; Peathegee Inc; **U2:** slavemotion/E+; **U3:** Marcel Weber/Cultura; Jose Luis Pelaez Inc/DigitalVision; nortonrsx/iStock/Getty Images Plus; Tara Moore/DigitalVision; Pekic/E+; Maskot; Image Source, **U4:** Andrea Comi/Moment; Enrique Díaz/7cero/Moment; izusek/E+; **U5:** © Philippe LEJEANVRE/Moment; Maskot; **U6:** HRAUN/E+; Maskot; sturti/E+; **U7:** Soft_Light/iStock/Getty Images Plus; pastie/E+; GrapeImages/E+; Maskot; **U8:** Morsa Images/DigitalVision; Plume Creative/DigitalVision; Carlina Teteris/Moment; Westend61; George Marks/Retrofile RF; **U9:** andresr/E+; Westend61; lechatnoir/E+; Rosmarie Wirz/Moment Open; **U10:** Prasit photo/Moment; Tooga/Photodisc; Gary Yeowell/DigitalVision; Daniele Sciarretta/EyeEm; **U11:** PeopleImages/E+; ViewStock; Westend61; **U12:** Hinterhaus Productions/DigitalVision; Westend61; Stígur Már Karlsson/Heimsmyndir/E+; Ivan/Moment; **U13:** MoMo Productions/DigitalVision; Balazs Sebok/iStock Editorial/Getty Images Plus; **U14:** Andersen Ross Photography Inc/DigitalVision; Izzet Keribar/The Image Bank Unreleased; Peter Cade/Stone; omersukrugoksu/iStock Unreleased;

Front cover photography by Howard Kingsnorth/Stone/Getty Images.

Illustration

Zacharias Papadopoulos (Hyphen S.A.)

Audio

Audio production by IH Sound Ltd.

Typesetting

Typeset by Hyphen S.A.